RAISING YOUR
Emotional
Intelligence

A Practical Guide

JEANNE SEGAL, Ph.D.

AN OWL BOOK

HENRY HOLT AND COMPANY · NEW YORK

Henry Holt and Company, LLC / *Publishers since 1866*
115 West 18th Street / New York, New York 10011

Henry Holt® is a registered
trademark of Henry Holt and Company, LLC.

Library of Congress Cataloging-in-Publication Data

Segal, Jeanne, date
Raising your emotional intelligence: a practical guide / Jeanne Segal. —
1st ed.
p.   cm.
"An Owl book."
Includes index.
ISBN 0-8050-5151-1
1. Emotions.   2. Emotions and cognition.   3. Emotions—Social
aspects.   4. Emotions—Problems, exercises, etc.   I. Title.
BF561.S43   1997
152.4—dc21   97-7453

Henry Holt books are available for special promotions
and premiums. For details contact: Director, Special Markets.

First Owl Books Edition 1997

Designed by Victoria Hartman

Printed in the United States of America

3   5   7   9   10   8   6   4

*To my sweet, kind, loving, beautiful,
and greatly talented daughter
Morgan Leslie, who in losing her passion
for life lost her desire to live it*

Contents

Part 3 · STAYING SMART

Acknowledgments

What comes out of us is always the work of many people. Certainly this is true of *Raising Your Emotional Intelligence*. The collaboration with my editor, Christine Benton, has been a labor of love. Her skill, wit, and heart guided and uplifted me time and again and helped craft a complex book aimed at addressing many needs. Thanks without measure to my wonderful husband, Robert, whose love, support, patience, and technical assistance I could not have done without. Thanks also to Jody Rein, my agent, for her brilliant guidance, and to David Sobel, my editor at Holt, for his critical input.

RAISING YOUR

Emotional
Intelligence

Introduction

Emotions matter. According to a mounting body of evidence, feeling is the most powerful resource we have. Emotions are life-lines to self-awareness and self-preservation that deeply connect us to ourselves and others, to nature and the cosmos. Emotions inform us about things that are of utmost importance to us—the people, values, activities, and needs that lend us motivation, zeal, self-control, and persistence. Emotional awareness and know-how enable us to recover our lives and our health, preserve our families, build loving and lasting relationships, and succeed in our work.

Since the early nineties, funds have been pouring out of research coffers for study of emotion's role in our lives. Compelling support for the importance of feeling in intelligence and well-being has started to appear in popular books and other media outlets. So far, though, we have not been offered a way to make emotion one of our tools for learning about ourselves and navigating a fulfilling course through our world.

Raising Your Emotional Intelligence is intended to fill that gap. Founded in my work and study over the last thirty years, it presents a practical method for returning our ability to feel to its rightful place alongside our ability to think. It is based on my belief that when we let ourselves feel our emotions fully and physically, as we're designed to do, we tap parts of the brain that have been lying dormant and gain the potential for keeping our intelligence growing for life.

My interest in the power of emotion began during the 1960s, when I was a young psychologist sitting on the board of the Association for Humanistic Psychology, coordinating its national conferences. Inspired by the feeling-centered theories, philosophies, and techniques of pioneers like Abraham Maslow, Rollo May, and Carl Rodgers, I eventually became one of the first practitioners in the country to specialize in holistic health. During the 1970s I was part of an early research effort by the Center for the Healing Arts involving cancer patients at UCLA that asked whether emotions played a role in the healing process. The resounding yes produced by our studies cemented my commitment to the exploration of emotion.

The long-term survivors I was studying had strong, clear ties to all their emotions. They knew what they felt and were not fearful or intimidated by strong emotions—theirs or other people's. Most important, this connection to their feelings informed, motivated, and activated their lives, drawing them toward others in spite of their own pain and suffering. Emotions also informed and guided the spiritual relationships that many survivors spoke of as an essential part of their healing.

Moved by these survivors, I threw myself into exploring the emotional resources that had contributed to their recovery. When I oversaw the investigations of a half-dozen graduate students into the characteristics of long-term survival, three traits surfaced: the ability to know what you feel; the ability to accept or be comfortable with all the feelings you identify, no matter their intensity; and the ability to act on this emotional information. From this point on, the question that became the passionate focus of my own work was: Since most of us don't have these skills, how do we develop them?

The answer, I was convinced, lay in the body. As I had grown more interested in the subject of emotions, the field of psychology had grown less interested. Emotion had become the "bad guy" of mental health and was denigrated, blunted, and generally ignored as a source of health and healing. Not only was feeling-centered therapy eventually replaced by cognitive therapies, but medication seemed to be the new focus of all health care. Medical treatments were directed at numbing physical pain, and psychological treatments were aimed at numbing emotional activity. To reclaim emotion as the powerful healing resource it is, it seemed to me we had to reclaim the ability to feel our emotions in the body.

So, for the next fifteen years, I explored and developed new possibilities for expanding emotional awareness through physical sensation and improving emotional management through my work in physicians' offices, clinics, hospitals, hospices, private practice, training programs, workshops, seminars, and through my writings. When I began to take a leadership role in a variety of nonprofit community-based institutions, it became clear that the emotional skills I had developed for use in the health field were also invaluable in all social and work settings. With the tragic death of my middle child I personally experienced how awareness of ourselves and others at an emotional level profoundly influences personal and social outcomes.

These observations and experiences inspired me to add my voice to the growing chorus of those who are again interested in exploring our emotional world. *Raising Your Emotional Intelligence* gives me an opportunity to share a life-sustaining and empowering gift that gives life its zest, hope, and meaning. I hope you will use this book to make emotional intelligence a permanent part of your life.

1

It's Smart to Feel

Why doesn't anybody like Lucy Leroy? As she'll be quick to tell you, she's smart, conscientious, well organized, and industrious. She cares about other people; she really does. But time after time, when the invitations go out, her name is left off the list; she hears chitchat of lunch plans in the making at the office but eats alone at her desk.

And whatever happened to Tom O'Brian? Tom was the kid in the neighborhood all the moms envied—so smart he got sent to a school for gifted kids; so creative his inventions won science prizes usually reserved for much older children. He was awarded a scholarship to some Ivy League school, but lately a rumor's been circulating that he dropped out and is repairing toasters out of his apartment. Could it be possible?

How about you? How's your life going? Have you achieved all you expected you would? Are you content with the number and depth of your friendships? Is your marriage the fountain of intimacy and support you dreamed it would be? Have you been promoted with the alacrity you deserve at work? Do you feel generally at ease in the world—or a little out of synch, for reasons you can't quite discern?

If you feel out of synch; if you answered no to many of the questions above, I can diagnose your problem in a snap. You're normal. You, Lucy, Tom—and Dick and Harry and Jane and

Joan—are average, red-blooded, thinking Americans, trained in family, school, and work to value the intellect and devalue the emotions, to squelch passion and to use your head to "figure out" what your body is feeling, to be, in short, smart—not emotional.

But what exactly is "smart" and at what cost do we stifle the emotional component of our identities?

I say the price is far too high, for ignoring our emotions leaves all of us—at least to some degree—lacking the skills we need to lead healthy, satisfying, fulfilling lives. Our IQ may help us understand and deal with the world on one level, but we need our emotions to understand and deal with ourselves and, in turn, others. Without an awareness of our emotions, without the ability to recognize and value our feelings and act in honest accordance with those feelings, we cannot get along well with other people, we cannot get ahead in the world (regardless of how "smart" we are), we cannot make decisions easily, and we are often simply at sea, out of touch with our sense of self.

Culturally, Americans (along with those of many other Western societies) have been taught to think of consciousness itself as an intellectual activity rather than as a heart or gut response. We've learned not to trust our emotions; we've been told emotions distort the allegedly more accurate information our intellect supplies. Even the term *emotional* signifies weak, out of control, even childish. "Don't be a baby!" we say to the little boy who is crying on the playground; "Leave him alone! Let him work it out!" we admonish the little girl who runs to help the little boy. In fact, we tend to mold our entire self-image around our intellect. Our abilities to memorize and problem-solve, to spell words and do mathematical calculations are easily measured on written tests; those measurements are slapped onto report cards in the form of grades and ultimately dictate which college will accept us and which career paths we should follow. If we do not perform well on these standardized tests, we clearly feel the impact of the label—any goal we have becomes that much tougher to reach when we know we may well not be smart enough to attain it.

Does your instinct tell you there's something wrong with that picture? That's because as much as our society tells us that being objective and rational is the way to get ahead, the sense that people weren't meant to be thinking-only beings runs strong in us all. When we see a film that moves us, we agree it was wonderful; when we see someone act with compassion, we applaud him or her. But we accept our emotionality only in the proper contexts: it's OK to cry at the movies but not on the job; it's fine to trust your gut playing poker but not when it comes to picking a product to market. Therein is the paradox. We are told to value the head and devalue the heart; instinctively, we value the heart and feel wrong for doing so. *We are not wrong.*

The Heart and the Head: Not So Separate After All

In studying people with strokes, brain tumors, and other types of brain damage, scientists have recently made some fascinating discoveries about intelligence. When the parts of our brains that enable us to feel emotions are damaged, our intellects remain intact. We can still talk, analyze, perform excellently on IQ tests, and even predict how one should act in social situations. But under these tragic circumstances we are unable to make decisions in the real world, to interact successfully with other people and/or to act appropriately, to plan for the immediate or long-term future, to reason, or finally to succeed.*

The exact neurological workings are not yet clear, but the brain-imaging technologies that are now helping scientists "map the human heart" suggest that the rational and emotional parts of the brain depend on each other.†

---

* Antonio Damasio, *Descartes' Error: Emotion, Reason and the Human Brain* (New York: Grosset/Putnam, 1994).
† Daniel Goleman, *Emotional Intelligence* (New York: Bantam, 1995).

In evolutionary terms our emotional facility is the more ancient, having existed in the primitive human brain stem well before the thinking part of the brain—the neocortex—even began to develop above it. Even more telling, though, is the fact that the centers of emotion in the brain continued to evolve right along with the neocortex and are now woven throughout that part of the brain, where they wield tremendous power over *all* brain functions. Could it be that emotion is meant to have more control of thought than thought has over emotion? Just a few years ago such a suggestion would have been scoffed at by scientists. But then along came Joseph LeDoux of New York University, who in the early nineties discovered that in fact the messages from our senses—our eyes, our ears—are first registered by the brain structure most heavily involved in emotional memory—the amygdala—before moving into the neocortex.

This means emotional intelligence actually *contributes* to rational thought. Which is why, physiologically, when the emotional centers of our brains are harmed, our overall intelligence is short-circuited. However, we don't need to suffer brain damage to rob our intellect of its essential emotional partner. We pay so little heed to our feelings now that our emotional resources have atrophied, like any unused muscle.

A Name for Emotional Smarts: EQ

Emotion and intellect are two halves of a whole. That's why the term recently coined to describe the intelligence of the heart is *EQ*. EQ is deliberately reminiscent of the standard measure of brainpower, IQ. IQ and EQ are synergistic resources: without one the other is incomplete and ineffectual. IQ without EQ can get you an A on a test but won't get you ahead in life. EQ's domain is personal and interpersonal relationships; it is responsible for your self-esteem, self-awareness, social sensitivity, and social adaptability.

When your EQ is high, you are able to experience feelings fully as they happen and truly get to know yourself. Keeping the lines of communication wide open between the amygdala and the neocortex thus endows you with compassion, empathy, adaptability, and self-control.

EQ provides a critical edge in work, family, social, romantic, and even spiritual settings; emotional awareness brings our inner world into focus. It enables us to make good choices about what to eat, whom to marry, what job to take, and how to strike a mutually healthy balance between our own needs and the needs of others.

Getting Back to Lucy

All of this may sound right—but does it feel a bit empty? That's because while I've told you what EQ can bring, I haven't engaged *your* emotions in the process. I've supplied words for your intellectual understanding. Now I'd like to try to hook your empathy by taking a closer look at how a low EQ gets in the way of so many of our day-to-day lives, out here in the real world.

Lonely People Who Need People: Why People with a Low EQ Push Other People Away

There are reasons Lucy is not on anybody's guest list. Lucy is a very angry woman. Maybe she's mad she didn't get promoted; maybe she's furious that her mother loved her sister more than her—we don't need to explore her reasons. (As we'll see, you don't need in-depth analysis to raise your EQ.) But Lucy doesn't want to know she's angry. Most of Lucy's focus is pushing away her feelings. And she's good at it. She numbs herself to her own feelings through constant mental chatter: "No one ever gives me a chance . . . They're so unfair . . . It wasn't *my* fault." She pushes those feelings right out—and right on to everyone else.

Because Lucy is unaware of both her own feelings and the feelings of others, she is always caught off guard and hurt by direct confrontations. She is therefore always *on* guard. Lucy defends herself at every turn—if you say the room feels warm, she'll tell you she was nowhere near the thermostat. When something upsets Lucy—and most things upset Lucy—it is a complete surprise to her, and her knee-jerk response is "I've done nothing wrong."

People sense the anger that Lucy tries to evade and get a vague feeling they'd rather not hang around her. Meanwhile, rather than experience the pain of consistent rejection, Lucy obsesses endlessly about how unfairly she is treated—and so perpetuates the cycle.

Lucy's EQ 101 Lesson:
Our thoughts obscure our feelings and the crucial
information that emotion provides.

As we'll explore throughout this book, there is a major difference between experiencing our feelings and thinking about them. Most of us are neophytes at the former, laureates at the latter. Lucy intellectualizes about her feelings all the time, shifting from feeling to thinking so quickly that she doesn't even realize she has crossed a line. She broods, she wallows; she rationalizes and rehearses, and in doing so all she does is change the emotion she experiences from internal hurt into inappropriate, poorly hidden rage.

Through the techniques in this book Lucy can learn to remain aware of all her feelings and not be caught off guard by emotional exchanges. A higher EQ would give her the ability to stay connected to herself even as she takes note of the feelings of others. This ability would permit her to hear unpleasant things without becoming defensive and to feel hurt without expressing that hurt as hostility. Lucy would become a much more desirable person to be around.

Low EQ + High IQ = Repairing Toasters:
Why Smart Folks Get Lost

I don't know why Tom ended up repairing toasters, but I'd bet he got there very soon after he experienced his first emotional setback. Maybe his father walked out on the family; maybe his first love dumped him for a football player. Whatever it was, it destroyed his confidence in a snap, because his entire identity was wrapped around the fragile and unpredictable trait of intellect.

Our intellectual abilities are innate and largely unchangeable. For very smart kids, good grades come naturally. It is therefore often hard to develop a strong sense of self-esteem when you are constantly rewarded for something that seems to be a transient gift. It came easily—and perhaps could go just as easily. People like Tom, who were in all likelihood encouraged to value only their intellectual achievements at the expense of their inner selves, end up with little fundamental sense of how they feel and therefore who they are. They are devastated by their first emotional setback, with little or no ability to handle the emotional fallout of even a minor failure. They do not know who they are if they are not the smartest kid in town. They feel lost and often end up getting lost, taking unchallenging jobs, giving up and dropping out.

Tom's EQ 101 Lesson:
Without EQ, IQ will always fall short.

Expecting to ride through life on the coattails of a high IQ alone is like expecting to be handed your first driver's license after only a written test. IQ predicts only how we'll do on paper, how we measure up to standards set by someone else. EQ helps us set our *own* standards.

That's because EQ illumines our inner world. People who are emotionally intelligent know the difference between what's important to them and what's important to someone else; they also know the difference between what they need to survive and a passing whim. Most important, they can weather life's thousands of setbacks. They have a sense of proportion that the "brainiest" among us often lose at a young age.

Low EQ on the Job = Middle Management Forever

Ladies and gentlemen, meet Henry. Henry is a brilliant accountant with an IQ of 160. Henry spends much of his day at his desk, sweating out figures in a race against himself and succeeding often enough to go home a little early. Henry spends much of his evenings complaining to his wife: "My boss has an IQ of 90. He has no idea what I do! My coworkers never give me the support I need to get things done right." This is all true. Is it unjust? Henry thinks so, and so does his ulcer.

What Henry hasn't told his wife is that his work is unimpressive in the ways that really matter. He's oblivious to the fact that he's a lousy troubleshooter who gets so bogged down in detail he rarely sees the big picture. He also doesn't see his boss grimace when he hands her unnecessarily technical and complex reports that are a painful struggle to decipher. It doesn't occur to him that everyone sees him leave early at least once a week, but no one's around to notice how often he comes in early because his ulcer often wakes him up before the alarm.

Henry doesn't see why he should spend any time worrying about other people's feelings. After all, he never gets any sympathy from them when, year after year, he's passed over for promotion, does he?

Henry's EQ 101 Lesson:
While thinking certainly interferes with feeling,
feeling does not interfere with thinking.

Intellect alone cannot help Henry—or any of us—navigate the choppy political and psychological waters of an office full of people, each with a different set of needs and desires. It takes empathy to second-guess a boss and learn which projects really carry the most corporate weight; to see a secretary's tension and not overload her with work on that particular day; to sense a client's dissatisfaction with your team's work despite his protestations to the contrary.

Though our cultural prejudices tell us otherwise, emotional acceptance supports our ability to reason effectively. Were Henry to follow the principles of this book and learn to raise his EQ, he would find his intellectual accomplishments expanded and his social skills enhanced. Secure in his ability to perceive and respond to his own emotional needs, Henry can risk reaching out and responding to the needs of others. In doing so, he will get ahead—big time. And maybe do something about that ulcer in the process.

When You Know How You Feel, You Know How You Feel
Sandy can't make up her mind. When she goes out to dinner, she orders "whatever everybody's having." She falls in love at the drop of a hat, unfortunately often with two men at once. Her relationships are passionate and short-lived. When pressed about her indecisiveness, she bursts into tears. "I just don't know what I want!" she yells.

Sandy is certainly emotional, but like so many low-EQ people, she hasn't really learned to trust her full range of feelings. When she doesn't like how she feels, she tries to cast it off by acting out her emotions—but her feelings remain tied to her intellectual expectations of what she should do and how she should act. She knows she should find a mate, so she ignores her heart's messages that she's with the wrong men. She knows everything there is to know about what to order in a restaurant (low-fat, skip the veal, go-ahead indulge, keep the price down, know the wine, skip the wine), but that knowledge gives her no clue as to what she really wants. Her head spins, and she just feels like crying.

Sandy's EQ 101 Lesson:
Decision making is a key benefit of raising your EQ.

While intellect can tell us many things objectively, it can't tell us how we feel, and it's our feelings that make our decisions wise.

Passive or Paralyzed: It's All in Your Head
Frank's wife would love it if he would just remember to take out the garbage. Frank's boss would love it if he would just take out a little initiative and call a meeting when a problem arises instead of waiting for someone else to point it out. Frank's kids would love it if he would just ask them, for once, to do something with him. Frank says he wishes he would do these things. He can see how easy they seem to others. He thinks about all the things he could or should do. And he doesn't do anything.

Frank's EQ 101 Lesson:
Intelligence helps us recognize a range of actions
but doesn't drive us to act; emotion does.

The root of the word *emotion* is the Latin *motere,* which means "to move." It is our emotions that release us from paralysis and motivate us to act. In fact, the more passionate we are about something, the more we are apt to act on it.

Moreover, studies have shown that we remember best those events that move us the most emotionally. People like Frank, who have closed themselves to the emotional significance of any action, often have a hard time simply remembering what they have promised to do.

Frank can see—coldly, clinically, logically—the sense in changing his ways. But until he masters the skills of active emotional awareness taught in this book, he'll remain distracted by intellectual demands, losing touch with the deep, strong feelings that drive the desire to act. By rooting us in a source of motivation that does not disappear as our interests shift, EQ keeps our determination fixed.

How Can Someone So Loud Be So Out of Touch?
Rod is an attractive man and an excellent dentist. But his temper is more painful to bear than a root canal. Despite his technical skills, he loses patients right and left. Maybe it's because

he rants and raves about the world's problems while clients squirm uncomfortably in his chair, or maybe it's more personal. For example, Rod attended to the dental needs of three members of the same family: father, mother, and college-age daughter. Rod inadvertently said something that offended the young woman. When the protective father brought the incident up, Rod slammed down his instruments and asked the man, through clenched teeth, how he could possibly know what had happened without having been there. This is not an emotionally intelligent response.

People with low EQs do have feelings, and those feelings do build to a point of being overwhelming at times. Indeed these people are more likely to become emotionally overwhelmed than people who consistently recognize the physical signals that herald emotion, because suppressed emotions, in time, can bubble to the surface, provoking physical ailments and causing unexpected emotional outbursts.

Rod distracts himself from feeling unpleasant feelings by blaming others—and hollering.

Rod's EQ 101 Lesson:
Feeling your emotions isn't a sign of weakness.

Because we've been told it's self-indulgent, most of us impose strict rules on how, when, where, and how much we allow ourselves to feel. If we cry at all, we don't do it in front of others. When we're angry, we bite our tongues. When we're hurt, we force a smile. But such actions backfire miserably for us all. It's healthy for mind, body, heart, and spirit to feel our feelings when they occur. Unexperienced feelings pop out, as we've seen in all of these examples, in self-destructive ways. If Rod adopts the techniques in this book, he'll discover that most strong feelings don't last long at all. Let them happen, and they leave us with a clear head, a contented heart, and greater self-control. Fight them, and they come back to haunt us.

High EQ = Infinite Possibilities

It's pretty clear how much easier life would be for us all if Lucy, Tom, Henry, Sandy, Frank, and Rod—and you and I—got an EQ boost. You can't feel at home in the world if you're not comfortable in your own skin. Once you are—once you've learned to accept your emotional self—every facet of your life can benefit:

• Thirteen-year-old Brent has started asking his parents to come to his junior high basketball games instead of pretending he doesn't know them now that Beth and Alan ask themselves, "How is our son feeling?" instead of "What was he *thinking?*"

• Anne now knows exactly when pleasing her aging parents begins to impose too much on her own needs. For the first time in her adult life, her parents are happy with all she gives, and Anne no longer has to feel guilty about "letting them down."

• Friends have noticed (with a twinge of envy) that Jeff and Barb are suddenly acting like new lovers—after twenty years of marriage. Their secret? They've put away the sex manuals and starting reading each other's feelings.

• They said it would never happen, but Sam is finally telling Jenny he wants less yardwork, more evenings out without the kids, and more control of the family checking account—and he's getting it.

Unless you know what you want, you can't ask for it.

Why EQ Is a Stronger Ally than IQ

As Sam learned, it's never too late to get what you want out of life. I believe we have EQ—not IQ—to thank for that fact. In fact, for any high-IQ disbelievers out there, here's one very objective reason to give EQ a hearty round of applause:

You can change your EQ.

You're stuck with your IQ forever.

Growing emotionally is a lifelong process, a beautiful part of our human potential. You can always learn to become aware of your feelings, to accept them, and to use the information they offer to the advantage of yourself and others. Time and again I've seen people of advanced age make great leaps in EQ. And the sky's the limit.

IQ is a different story. You were born with—or without—the capacity to develop math, linguistic, or other testable intellectual skills. How close you come to your intellectual potential may be affected by your environment or your EQ, but that potential is fixed, predetermined—a fact.

How much EQ you can develop over a lifetime is determined by only one thing—motivation. Fortunately, I've found EQ is kind of like golf: once you're hooked, you're compelled to keep trying to improve your game.

How to Get Smart

I know there are very clear ways to increase your EQ. I've used them myself and helped hundreds of clients and thousands of seminar attendees change their lives using the instruction and exercises that are now presented in this book.

Think of getting emotionally smart as another trip through school:

Step 1: Elementary School—Feeling Our Bodies' Feelings

When we enter emotional elementary school, we have little sense of our own bodies and therefore our own feelings. Yet we don't have to reach too deeply into our experience to recognize that all emotions are physical events. You can probably remember feeling serious fright as a pang in the pit of your stomach, sorrow as a heavy weight in your chest, joy as a euphoric swelling around your heart. The only feeling we have in our heads is a headache. So our elementary curriculum involves learning to recognize the feelings in our bodies by doing the exercises in chapter 3.

Step 2: High School—Accepting Those Feelings

Becoming aware of but not accepting your emotions is like getting into shape and then taking up smoking. What was the point? In chapter 4 I'll show you how to build the stamina that I call "emotional muscle" so you can live with what you've found out about your feelings—especially how to cut off the intellect when it inevitably tries to intrude and distort the emotional messages you're receiving.

Step 3: College—Hanging in There

You can get pretty adept at using those skills of emotional awareness and acceptance within the hallowed halls of your high school (kind of like winning at *Jeopardy* from your living room), but now rivalries become intense, relationships blossom, responsibilities multiply: You're in college, away from home for the first time. You need a way to hold on to the tools you've acquired now that you're out there in the halls of life.

Developing *active* emotional awareness—fully experiencing every emotion we feel every day—and using it along with our powers of cognition to set a course in life takes acute sensitivity. I'll show you how to turn emotional awareness into a lifetime habit in chapter 5.

Graduation with Bonus Points

The benefits of a high EQ ripple outward in ever-widening circles. Simply put, those who care for themselves can also care for others. So your bonus for recognizing and accepting your feelings and withstanding all the external pressures to ignore them is great empathy. In chapter 6 we'll learn to strike a balance between caring for others and caring for ourselves.

How Much Emotional Muscle Do You Already Have?

As I've said, anyone can get into this school at any time. But it always helps to know where you stand from the start. So let's begin by gauging the emotional muscle you're bringing to the classroom.

◦◦ QUIZ ◦◦

A Brief Entrance Exam

Pop quiz! Take this quiz quickly—no thinking allowed. Fill in the following statements with *never, rarely, sometimes, frequently,* or *always*. Answer as rapidly as possible; don't pause to flex your intellectual muscle!

1. Feeling left out or ignored troubles me.
   (never, rarely, sometimes, frequently, always)
2. When I have done something I'm ashamed of, I can admit it.
   (never, rarely, sometimes, frequently, always)
3. It upsets me when a stranger is less than friendly to me.
   (never, rarely, sometimes, frequently, always)
4. I can laugh at my vulnerabilities.
   (never, rarely, sometimes, frequently, always)
5. I beat myself up for making mistakes.
   (never, rarely, sometimes, frequently, always)
6. I can recognize my imperfections without feeling guilty.
   (never, rarely, sometimes, frequently, always)
7. When someone gets angry at me, it spoils my day.
   (never, rarely, sometimes, frequently, always)
8. I experience a full range of feeling every day, including sadness, anger, and fear.
   (never, rarely, sometimes, frequently, always)

9. My intense emotions cause me to feel out of control.
   (never, rarely, sometimes, frequently, always)
10. I agonize over decisions or put off decision making.
    (never, rarely, sometimes, frequently, always)
11. Other people's intense emotions cause me to feel out of control.
    (never, rarely, sometimes, frequently, always)

How did you do? If your EQ is nearing its full potential, you probably answered "never" or "rarely" to the odd-numbered questions and "always" or "frequently" to the even-numbered questions. But before you start to picture yourself smugly handing this book back to the well-meaning friend who gave it to you, please bear with me for just a few more questions:

Did you take the test quickly? If you agonized over your answers (and the possible implications for your own deficient character) or tried to "psych out" the test by answering the way you think you should, your intellect is firmly in control, your emotional muscle pretty flabby. (Yes, Henry the accountant finished quickly, but only thanks to incredible mental speed. And yes, after reading the preceding paragraph, he handed the book back to his wife, who had bought it for him.)

Do you think the test is stupid? The urge to disown our (possibly incriminating) feelings can be so strong that your first and lasting reaction may have been scorn for the oversimplification of this modest little quiz. You're not ready to suspend disbelief and just see what your emotions can tell you. (Lucy got so involved in an imaginary confrontation in which I was shamed into admitting I had set up this quiz only to make her look stupid that she never even got to question 3.)

Did you go back and change any of your answers? Rod started out answering "never" to the odd-numbered questions and "always" to the others. Then he got up from his desk, got a cup of coffee, returned, and erased his answers, replacing all of his *nevers* with either "rarely" or "sometimes." After "proofreading" his test once more, he agitatedly scratched out his answers, replaced all of them with "sometimes," then tore the page out of this book, crumpled it up, and stomped out of his office.

Obviously you're not alone if the quiz showed your intellect is in control. I'll explain why we're all in that boat in chapter 2. But even if you think you aced this quiz, your answers may not have come from the heart, despite your intentions. What's more important for now is how you felt about taking the test and how you feel now. Even unpleasant discoveries you've made, like how much pressure you place on yourself for silly reasons, are opportunities for emotional growth. Grab whatever chances you get. You're in the door and on your way to higher emotional learning!

Looking Ahead:
What Your Diploma Will Bring

All this is not to say there is no risk in raising your EQ. The price we pay for the information about ourselves that emotions bring forth is that it often conflicts with sacred beliefs about how secure we feel or how pleased we are with various choices we have made. Many of us would rather not be aware of our vulnerability and culpability.

Then why do we take the risk? Because safety comes at the price of loneliness, isolation, and stress. But even more because EQ heightens the highs. Studies have shown that we can feel only as high as we can feel low. If we're willing to learn to recognize and feel our most frightening anger, our most distressing sadness, our scariest fears, we stand to reap no less than ecstasy. As you will see in chapters 7, 8, and 9, these lessons give us unlimited potential for enhancing love, work, and family life.

So I invite you to join me as we enter the school of the heart. I promise you that following the exercises in this book will help you weather life's invariable emotional setbacks, understand how others feel and why they may respond to you in distressing ways, make up your mind, avoid inappropriate emotional outbursts, raise emotionally healthy children, and feel in synch with the world. Big promise?

Feeling is believing.

2

Why Johnny (and Jenny) Can't Feel

Johnny and Jenny can't feel because they're afraid to, and so, probably, are you. In the middle of an ordinary day you suddenly notice a sharp pang in your stomach, an alarming flutter in your chest, or a dull ache around your heart. What do you do?

If you're like most of us, your automatic reaction is to try to make the feeling stop. Maybe you let loose a barrage of mental chatter. Or you clench your teeth and think about something else. Possibly you turn on the TV for distraction (you'd call it diversion) and reach for the bowl of candy or glass of wine at your side.

And you do all of this without realizing it. Most of us have been so frightened of our feelings for so long that we cut them off before the mind registers them. If asked, in fact, we'd all claim to be feeling, caring, sensitive people. We think we feel, but we don't.

That's why this chapter is devoted to demonstrating that you, just like the rest of us, have developed a large repertoire of ways to use the mind to suppress the heart's messages. A series of quizzes will prove that you don't really feel, that instead you think about feeling. That's an important difference, because people who think instead of feel are diverted from what's really important to them—their deeply held values, the unique matrix of emotions that makes up their personality—and therefore end up *acting* like someone else.

How you act is what really matters to you, isn't it? We'd all like to walk through our world with personal integrity, with a generous benevolence toward our fellow citizens, reaching our goals and nourishing our spirit. That's not possible when we lose touch with our feelings, yet we believe it's just the opposite: that our feelings will make fools of us because they'll make us behave inappropriately if we don't keep them under wraps. The final quiz in this chapter will show how false that belief is, indicating where your EQ stands based on how you act in certain situations and where your emotional strengths lie.

With that information in hand you'll be motivated to enter the school of the heart. With the few transitional exercises in this chapter you'll also be well prepared to reawaken your sleeping emotions.

That alarm you're hearing is your heart begging to be heard. Isn't it time you listened?

To begin, here's a little aptitude test.

↘ QUIZ ↙

Measuring Your Emotional Aptitude

Fill in all the blanks within 90 seconds. Don't think—just write. If you have a timer handy, set it to begin now.

1. I am much too _____.
2. I should _____.
3. If I cared about _____, I would _____.
4. I always notice how badly I _____ and _____.
5. I'm not _____ enough.
6. My _____ is too _____.
7. Whenever I _____, I punish myself by _____.
8. I shouldn't _____ so often.
9. I'm always disappointed with _____.
10. Compared to _____, I'm _____.

11. Men are _____ and they should _____.
12. Women are _____ and they should _____.
13. Growing older is _____.
14. Young people are _____ and they should _____.
15. Republicans are _____ and they should _____.
16. Democrats are _____ and they should _____.
17. Liberals are _____ and they should _____.
18. The Religious Right is _____ and should _____.
19. The media is _____ and should _____.
20. I am _____ and should _____.

Let's see how you did.

1. Did the test take you less than 90 seconds? If so, you show a willingness to turn off your mind and tap in to the other resources that spur you to action. Good for you—that's the first step toward awakening your emotions.

2. Did it make you laugh? I hope so, because a sense of humor will short-circuit mental machinations every time.

3. Can you read your answers without cringing over what they may reveal about you? Congratulations on your courage—I think you're ready to find out what you've been missing all these years.

If you did cringe, don't blame yourself. Every single person I know who has taken this quiz has found the voice of criticism or judgment creeping in somewhere, and it's not a pretty sound. It is, however, only natural. For years, our culture has taught us to shun the compassionate heart and embrace the critical mind.

We all have a lot to unlearn.

Emotional Lessons of the Tender Years

It's no wonder you're afraid to feel. Childhood messages that our feelings are somehow unworthy only affirm the primordial instinct to cut off the palpable pain of anger and sorrow, despair and fear. We end up filled with shame over our feelings, with a pile of bad emotional memories on top. Then we perpetuate our fear of feeling into adulthood by using our heads to explain it all away: The reason we shouldn't feel is that emotion is dangerous. Where did the cycle begin for you?

❧ QUIZ ❧

Home Is Where the Heart Is—Or Is It?

We all tend to cover up the fact that it didn't feel too good when our well-intentioned parents made us ashamed of our feelings. We try to protect ourselves from feeling hurt today by joking about autocratic messages like "Because I *said* so!" and "I'll give you something to cry about!" The truth is we *are* still hurting because of such messages. So I want you to recall the refrains you heard throughout your childhood. That's one of the best ways I know to trace your antifeeling orientation to its origin.

Mom always said, "_____."
Dad always said, "_____."

1. Write a list of these phrases on a sheet of paper.
2. Do the same for those unmistakable looks your parents and other close adult relatives gave you.
3. Now review your lists. Check off all the items that made a negative comment about emotion in general.
4. Now check off all the items that were directed specifically at something you *did* but made you feel ashamed of who you *are*.
5. Compare the number of checks from steps 3 and 4 with the total number of refrains on your lists.

Did you check off more than half the items listed? I wouldn't be surprised, because antifeeling messages are everywhere. But also we tend to remember emotional hurts longer than other events, and when your EQ is low you're not even aware that emotions from your past keep intruding on the present. This quiz probably opened your eyes to a surprising degree of shame that was instilled in you by your parents, no matter how nice and loving they were.

Hold on to that piece of paper—you'll need it again in chapter 9.

☜ QUIZ ☞

Can You Fit In Without Falling Apart?

Even if your home was an emotional haven, there was always a wider world—of school, friends, and community—and you got plenty of messages about feelings out there as well. Whether those messages affirmed the validity of your feelings and made you feel worthy and welcome is reflected in how well you feel you fit in today. Rank yourself on a scale of 1 to 10 for the following qualities, from 1 for those least true of you to 10 for most true.

1. I always follow the rules.

1   2   3   4   5   6   7   8   9   10

2. I always enjoy organized activities—clubs, associations, etc.

1   2   3   4   5   6   7   8   9   10

3. I'm a perfectionist.

1   2   3   4   5   6   7   8   9   10

4. I like to plan everything far in advance.

1   2   3   4   5   6   7   8   9   10

5. I take risks whenever I can.

1   2   3   4   5   6   7   8   9   10

6. I never get embarrassed when I make a mistake.

1   2   3   4   5   6   7   8   9   10

7. I'd rather lead than follow.

1   2   3   4   5   6   7   8   9   10

8. Wherever I go, I usually feel like I don't fit in.

1   2   3   4   5   6   7   8   9   10

9. In group settings, the common good is always most important to me.

1   2   3   4   5   6   7   8   9   10

10. I never show my true feelings in public.

1   2   3   4   5   6   7   8   9   10

If you gave yourself a 5 for each item, you know that it makes sense to lead in some arenas and follow in others, to follow the rules as long as they don't violate your personal values, and to extend forgiveness to everyone—including yourself—for the inevitable human flaws. You have a high EQ—either because the society and culture you grew up in accepted you wholeheartedly on your own terms or because you came from such a high-EQ home that you were able to fend off anti-emotion messages from outside.

It's more likely, though, that your ratings fell to one end or the other of the scale in some cases, showing that you either don't trust society or don't trust yourself. Hold on to this quiz while I explain.

"Shame on You . . ."

It's so easy to fall prey to shame. When you took the "Home Is Where the Heart Is" quiz, you probably listed stock phrases like "Children should be seen and not heard," "Don't get mad; get even," and "You're so much prettier when you smile." Statements like these make us feel ashamed of having "unpleasant" emotions like anger and sadness; they tell us that whatever feelings we have, they aren't worth hearing about.

Then there are criticisms of our behavior that we heard as criticisms of our feelings: "Don't laugh so loud; they'll hear you." "It's not polite to stare." "Go to your room until you can calm down." These too made us feel ashamed of ourselves and our emotions because the adults in our lives probably didn't take care to distinguish between unacceptable actions and acceptable feelings. How could you be sure Mom was furious just because you punched Billy when he wouldn't give your truck back? Maybe she disapproved of your getting angry at Billy for taking the toy in the first place.

Best to be on the safe side and throw out the feelings along with the behavior—a choice heartily approved by all the social institutions outside the house. When our schools, religions, and others drummed rules into us and set rigid standards for social acceptance, they were saying that our emotions are not to be trusted. In fact, they echoed what we heard from our parents: "Take it like a man," said your football coach. "Keep smiling if you expect to be loved," said pictures of women in your favorite magazine.

No wonder, as the preceding quiz showed, so many adults today either follow rules to the letter or reject them wholesale. They have no confidence in their ability to decide what's right for themselves; they can't respond to changing circumstances and conflicting needs with personal integrity because they don't trust the feedback their feelings provide. So if you did poorly on the quiz, it's because you're ruled by fear and shame instilled in part by society. EQ can change that.

The Memories That Haunt Us

Earlier I said that emotional hurts tend to stay with us, and that's why we carry our shame and fear into our adult lives. The emotional lessons we learn at a very early age make us feel worthless as children and keep us from thinking straight and acting wisely as adults, all because of one of the most primordial structures of the brain.

The emotional centers of the brain were originally intended to protect us from danger. By sending us a physically palpable— and distinctly unpleasant—message that something was wrong, they spurred us into whatever action would save our lives and thereby also stop that painful signal. Today our emotions still send us painful signals when we're sad or angry, but we no longer trust those messages. We're ashamed of what we feel, and as a result we're flooded with fear of those sensations. To assuage our fear we use the rational parts of the brain to cut off the feelings before the body is finished delivering its emotional message.

Whew, we think; we've stopped that awful feeling and we're home free.

Not so fast. The amygdala, our emotional memory bank, has already registered not only the original emotion and its cause but also the fear associated with that feeling. Now, whenever a similar event occurs, the amygdala sends out a louder and louder alarm. We're still spurred into action by the emotional part of the brain, but now we overreact or otherwise act inappropriately. Stored anger at your father gets dumped on an unsuspecting employer twenty years later—and gets you fired. Unresolved fear of being abandoned by your mother turns up as clingyness that drives away your wife—not once but three times.

To be blunt, letting emotional memories pile up in your brain like layers of dust on an old window makes you stupid. You can't handle the crises of today because you keep confusing them with the crises of yesterday. You never learn exactly what makes you happy or sad because you really don't know what happiness and sadness feel like.

If you want to clean off that grime so you can see clearly and act wisely, you need to conquer your fear of feeling. I'll tell you how in chapters 3 to 6, but you can get a headstart right now by practicing interrupting the fight-or-flight reflex.

HEADING OFF FEAR

When you're out there in the world and you feel some kind of discomfort that you can't put your finger on, when you feel a familiar urge to run away or you do something completely inappropriate like laugh when you really want to cry, stop yourself for just long enough to take a deep breath.

What do you feel in your chest, in your lower back, in your stomach, in your thighs, shoulders, neck, or jaw? A squeezing, as if something inside you is all knotted up? That's fear, and it doesn't have to conquer you—as long as you recognize it for what it is.

That's all there is to it—for now. This little exercise will give you confidence that you can control the way you act; you can relearn to feel and get smart.

Of course you've probably heard numerous logical reasons for fearing emotion. Such explanations have been offered up by psychology for decades, by literature and philosophy for centuries. As it turns out, they are largely myths. They don't hold up to neurological scrutiny or, in many cases, to logic, either. The following facts should support your efforts to practice interrupting the fear response to feeling.

Exposing the Myths About Emotion

1. Emotion is inferior, because it's more primitive than reason. There's no denying that the amygdala, the neurological seat of emotion, is a more ancient part of the evolving human brain than the neocortex, the seat of reason. But it's not more primitive. The emotional and rational parts of the brain have evolved together and, in fact, are intertwined, both structurally and biochemically, working together in a constant feedback loop. Through this cooperative mechanism we achieve not only primitive self-preservation but also sophisticated creativity, empathy, sociability, and boundless self-knowledge.

2. Emotion is dangerous. Yes, emotional pain hurts—a lot. But feeling it won't kill you. Quite the opposite, in fact. Years ago, at the Center for the Healing Arts, the first holistic health center in

Los Angeles, I headed a study linking survival with acceptance of intense emotion. The one factor survivors and potential survivors shared was their ability to experience a full range of intense emotions, including fear, rage, sadness, joy, and love. We also followed a group of healthy persons who reported a favorable relationship with their intense emotions and found that they had a better chance of remaining healthy than those who ignored or feared their emotions.

Just like physical pain, emotional pain is a warning, and it should be heeded. When it's not, emotional pain often becomes chronic physical pain. When people who suffer from migraine headaches are taught to recognize and address emotionally charged events, for example, the headaches often disappear.

3. Self-control comes from stifling feelings. The behavior we condemn as inappropriate and antisocial has more to do with silencing than expressing emotion. For example, studies discredit the popular notion that anger is responsible for the aggressive behavior supposedly released by drinking alcohol. Psychologist G. Alan Marlantt concludes that the link between alcohol and anger is social rather than physiological. People use alcohol as they use anger: as permission to do something they want to do. In cultures where aggressive behavior is not permitted, people drink heavily without becoming angry or abusive.

We don't expect to make good decisions without all the facts, yet we do expect to act wisely without the information that our feelings impart. Emotion is an irreplaceable resource; it tells us through instant physical feedback whether a decision or an action is right for us. Self-control does not come from controlling our feelings but from feeling our feelings.

4. There are good emotions and bad emotions. All emotions come from the same part of the brain, and you can't cut off the painful ones and still fully enjoy the pleasant ones. All emotions are good: They're all informative and often constructive. How often, for example, would wrongs be righted without the catalyst of anger? Similarly, emotional pain can be a reminder to wake up, to pay attention to something in your life that needs to be changed. Sadness and grief enable us to experience loss in a way that permits the rebirth of energy and enthusiasm for life. Raw fear, as distinguished from intellectualized thoughts about scary things, sparks lifesaving actions. All deeply felt emotions deliver messages we need to hear.

5. Emotion clouds your judgment. We do some of our best work with less input, not more, from the neocortex. Neurologists have found that the "flow" state in which we perform the most challenging tasks in a given area is marked by less cortical arousal than performance of mundane tasks. Then there's the mental boost we get from adrenaline ("butterflies") when nervous or afraid—provided we physically experience our emotions. When we constrict our bodies as we do when we cut off emotions, we block oxygen to the brain.

Raw emotion doesn't interfere with cognitive processes, but we believe it does because we mistake thinking about feelings for experiencing emotion. That's where we get into trouble: The mental busywork we engage in to avoid the physical experience of emotion diverts brainpower away from decision making and thus does cloud our judgment.

Mental Habits That Keep Us from Being Smart

Here are some of the most popular tricks we play on ourselves to keep our feelings in check. Take the quizzes that accompany them to discover which ones you favor; use the exercises in this section to begin nudging yourself toward feeling.

1. We daydream. As children we disguise helplessness and hopelessness by using the mind to establish imaginary controls.

When we feel hurt, discounted, abused, or left out, we produce comforting pictures of safety, self-importance, and belonging—daydreams that soothe or deaden troubling emotions. Many of us continue to use our minds in this way long after we grow up and are no longer helpless. When painful emotions arise, rather than feel our way through them we simply space out. We don't resolve our own problems, and we don't listen to the feelings of loved ones.

2. We rehearse and replay. When shame is deeply ingrained, our automatic response to feeling bad is to blame someone—usually ourselves. We gladly trade the unknown (what's really wrong) for the known (our unworthiness or someone's else's fault). Or we disguise distressing feelings as something more acceptable. Brooding over the curtains ruined by the dry cleaner, for example, lets us substitute anger for the fear of feeling vulnerable and helpless. This mental mischief ranges from briefly berating ourselves for our faults to rehashing and reliving events ad infinitum. Of course we learn nothing this way, no matter how many times we indulge in reruns or rehearsals.

How often do you lose yourself in mental chatter? The following exercise is remarkably revealing.

CLICKING IN TO SELF-SCOLDING

You can end up losing all connection with the living world if you let critical mental chatter go unchecked. Many of us start out with cryptic self-recriminations, but before long we're spending all our time rehashing and rehearsing life and none living it—all because we can't endure the emotions that living elicits. To make sure that doesn't happen to you, pick up one of those little clickers that golfers use to keep track of their strokes. Pocket-sized and inexpensive, they're great devices for effortlessly counting repetitive events.

1. Carry the clicker around with you for one to three days, clicking in every time you mentally scold yourself: "Why didn't

I . . . ?" "How could I be so dumb?" "How could I have said that?"

2. That's all you really have to do for now, but if you want to take another step, repeat the exercise, but this time stop whenever you click in and ask yourself, "In this moment, what am I experiencing emotionally?"

I can't predict how often you'll click in—most of us mentally scold ourselves about once an hour—but I guarantee it will be much more frequently than you'd ever guess. Awareness is half the battle, so this revelation alone can make you more forgiving of yourself. Keep up the exercise as long as you see a noticeable decrease in your number of daily clicks.

As for optional step 2, you may identify anger, embarrassment, or other unpleasant emotions. If the emotion you identified doesn't surprise you, its intensity in proportion to the stimulating event may. On the other hand, you may discover that fear is beneath all your self-blame—and that's a substantial step toward raising your EQ.

3. We classify and label. Slotting everything and everyone into neat little categories is a clever way to avoid relying on your own instincts. Since the time of Aristotle, Western thinking has been characterized by a dualistic approach to life that began with the separation of mind from body and flowed naturally into the juxtaposition of good against evil. This polar perspective forces us to classify everything as opposites, with one member of each pair being superior and the other inferior. You know how reason and feeling fall out. But are you aware of what you may be missing when you label everything according to some preconceived nomenclature? Your feelings don't put people or any other part of your world in permanent boxes; they give you nonjudgmental, unfettered feedback that keeps your potential for learning infinite.

❧ QUIZ ❧

Does Dualism Have a Hold on You?

Place each word in the following pairs of words in either the "Superior" or "Inferior" column:

	Superior	Inferior
body, mind		
sensual, intellectual		
feeling, thinking		
nature, culture		
physical, mental		
feminine, masculine		
weak, strong		
bad, good		
wrong, right		
poor, rich		
inner, outer		
left, right		
lower, higher		
earth, heaven		
old, young		
dark, light		
passion, reason		

If you finished this quiz rapidly and simply transferred all the words at the right to the "Inferior" column and all those at left to the "Superior" column, you're not likely to be open to the full range of information your emotions offer. You probably view life in black-and-white terms and may not learn too easily.

4. *We cite data and authority.* Sure, it's important to know the facts, but which do you really find persuasive—data or passion? Take Vic as an example. Vic lectures and occasionally pontificates but never, never says "I" as in "I want," "I need," or "I feel" (an

"I think" creeps into his lectures now and then). At meetings coworkers roll their eyes when he starts to drone on about statistics and risk-benefit ratios. No one is surprised that Vic's proposal for reengineering his company's manufacturing process has been turned down for the last three years—or that Vic's supervisor, Nora, just pushed it through by snatching up Vic's rejected proposal, marching up to the VP's desk, and making an impassioned plea for another review: "David, I feel strongly that we could save this company a lot of money and put out a better product if we adopted Vic's plan as soon as possible . . ."

Why are people like Vic everywhere? Three hundred and fifty years ago French philosopher and mathematician René Descartes uttered the immortal words "I think, therefore I am." Though Descartes himself never denied the importance of emotion, his point was exaggerated and distorted: Rational thought became synonymous with consciousness—the human self—and emotion was relegated to secondary status. Meanwhile the so-called scientific method made fact and logic, marked by objectivity, the ideals; anything personal—with emotion heading the list—was considered tainted by subjectivity.

Not much has changed in three centuries. Many people still believe credibility comes from abstraction and depersonalization. While they're gathering data, their passionate counterparts are winning friends and influencing people—but the IQ worshipers aren't sharp enough to notice.

❧ QUIZ ☙

Are You a Noncommittal Communicator?

People who don't invest their words with the passion they feel rarely get the response they were hoping for. Pick a place where you feel particularly vulnerable—for many of us, that's the workplace, but it could also be home or elsewhere—and spend a couple of days paying attention to how you communicate.

1. How often do you say "I feel"?

2. What do you do to make a point (or just provide a diversion) when you don't say "I feel"?

- Tell a story?
- Tell a joke?
- Quote an authority? ("They say . . ." "I've read . . ." "Statistics show . . ." "It's obvious that . . ." "My therapist says . . ." "My boss says . . ." "The Bible says . . .")
- Assume authority, as in "Everyone knows that the world is flat"?
- Send a "you" message, like "You must feel that everyone on welfare is picking your pocket"?
- Smile a lot?
- Try to be entertaining?

Many of us *never* say "I feel." You've got a modicum of EQ if you use the phrase at all, but unless you use it whenever you want someone to listen, you probably aren't getting much of what you want. What kind of reaction do you get to the tactics you do use? Is it the response you're really after? Probably not. In that case the following exercise will help.

REPLACING "I THINK" WITH "I FEEL"

When we say "I think so," we're expressing uncertainty. Isn't it odd, then, that we use "I think" to express strong opinions—and to communicate feelings? From now on, try to stop yourself when you're about to say "I think" and replace it with "I feel." Doing so should (1) imbue your statements with more conviction and thus make them much more persuasive and (2) deter you from saying things you don't really believe (and thus relieve you of the urge to rehash and obsess over what you should have said!). The effect will be gradual, but it will noticeably shift you from a pure-thought mode of communication to one that includes feeling.

How Not Feeling Translates
into Action (or Inaction)

We space out, we waste time on internal dialogue, we distance ourselves too far to understand others or wield any influence over them—and these mental gyrations are only half the story. When we refuse to feel our emotions, they take their toll—on our physical health and our social aplomb. Here's how.

1. Unfelt feelings make us ill. As children, we learn to tighten muscles around our eyes and lips, hold our breath, and squeeze viscera, muscles, and other tissue to disguise tears, conceal anger, and appear calm and unaffected. We minimize hurt or fear by clenching our teeth, sucking in our stomach, and applying pressure to the chest, shoulders, jaw, pelvis, and lower back. Shallow breathing helps us convert fear or hurt into anger and rage into sadness. Squeezing muscles in the lower body lets us force a smile. Unfortunately, the emotional pain we stave off in the short term usually returns as chronic physical pain in the long term.

"I grew up believing that emotion or at least emotional display was sinful," recalls Sharon. "I come from an ultra-religious family where 'making waves' offended God. The Lord, I was told, 'likes little girls to be quiet, helpful, generous, and studious.' It was devil's work when I was angry, hurt, sullen, or even sad, and, sure enough, when I was naughty, I got a headache. I don't believe anymore that the devil made me do it, but I get horrible migraine headaches."

❧ QUIZ ☙
Where Have Your Painful Feelings Gone?

If you still think you're a fully feeling human being, investigate how many of these chronic aches, pains, or illnesses have been yours.

- Stomachaches
- Migraine headaches
- Backaches
- Stiff neck

- Ulcers
- Frequent colds
- Asthma
- Insomnia

Any of these could be a sign of stuffed feelings insisting on being felt. The more of these afflictions you've suffered, the lower your EQ—and you're not likely to resolve them without raising your EQ.

2. Unfelt feelings make us compulsive. As we grow older, we learn to keep feelings like anger, grief, and fear in check by becoming absorbed in compulsive activities such as obsessive eating, studying, or daydreaming. Later we discover that emotions can be numbed by smoking, drinking, and taking drugs. In a culture whose mythology denigrates emotion and urges us to avoid pain, including emotional pain, the list of compulsive and addictive behaviors includes anything done consistently to excess, including working, watching TV, meditating, exercising, and socializing.

❧ QUIZ ❧

What Can't You *Stop* Doing?

What do you feel driven to do to excess though you know it's unhealthy, exhausting, or meaningless? Check off all that apply:

Smoking
Drinking
Drugs
Overworking
Overeating

Obsessive exercising
Obsessive meditating
Nonstop socializing
Other obsessive behavior

Don't be fooled by the good-for-you guise of some activities. Just because it's exercise doesn't mean it's physically or psychologically healthy to do it till you drop. When do you head for the gym, decide to do a little more work, or reach for the cookies? Paying attention to what trips your compulsive behavior will tell you what you're typically afraid of. To find out how effective this type of tactic is, explore how you feel afterward: as if you've resolved a knotty problem, or as if you're just exhausted, numb, and disappointed?

3. Unfelt feelings make us do and say the wrong thing at the wrong time—or do nothing at all. Without the self-knowledge that emotion provides, we do things we later regret, we lack the passion to act quickly and appropriately based on what's important to us, and we have no idea how to interact effectively with others. So, as much as we'd like to think that emotions are strictly internal, our feelings *will* out. Our EQ is evident in everything we do and say.

Ready for the acid test? You may think you're in touch with how you feel, but I bet your actions prove otherwise. Let's find out how high your EQ is.

✎ QUIZ ✐

Measuring Your EQ by Your Behavior

1. When someone important to you screams angrily at you, you:
   a. Immerse yourself in a daydream.
   b. Say you're sorry even when you're not.
   c. Say how upsetting it is to be yelled at.
   d. Begin a debate.
2. When you want a raise, you give your boss:
   a. A memo summarizing your terrific track record over the last year.
   b. A short verbal list of why it's really important to you.
   c. A salary survey published in the *New York Times*.
   d. An ultimatum.

3. When someone you respect humiliates you by making a crack in front of others about a mistake you've made, you:
   a. Go home and vow never to put yourself in such a vulnerable position again.
   b. Make a sharp comeback.
   c. Go home and write a letter explaining that you never made the mistake in the first place.
   d. Make light of it if you can and then privately tell the person how you felt.
4. A friend brings the light conversation at a dinner party to a dead halt by suddenly confessing to being on Prozac. You:
   a. Change the subject.
   b. Sympathetically relate how depressed you've been lately.
   c. Ask how your friend is feeling right now.
   d. Offer a good book on the subject.
5. A distraught employee bursts in with a complaint when you're already in the middle of a crisis. You:
   a. Ask for a memo on the problem and go back to your crisis.
   b. Mentally prepare your response while listening to keep the interruption brief.
   c. Stop what you're doing to look directly at your employee and ask how urgent it is.
   d. Call in someone else who's involved and delegate the problem.
6. When your child cries loud and long over a minor bump, you:
   a. Say "That must have hurt" and leave the child alone.
   b. Quietly say "You shouldn't make such a big deal out of a little bump."
   c. Say nothing and hold the child until he/she stops crying.
   d. Laugh and say "Oh, come on, big kids don't cry."
7. When you feel depressed, you:
   a. Ask whether it's a feeling you experience frequently.
   b. Ask why nobody ever seems to notice.
   c. Ask where the box of chocolates is.

    d. Ask why you should be unhappy when so many people are worse off.

8. When you need to concentrate for an extended period of time, you:

    a. Take your phone off the hook and make sure no one disturbs you.

    b. Make sure you're rested and physically relaxed.

    c. Have an extra cup of coffee.

    d. Warm up with some brainteasers.

9. When you're ill but people are counting on you to show up somewhere, you:

    a. Show up because you promised you would.

    b. Assume they'll get someone to fill in when you don't show up.

    c. Ask for help.

    d. Call and insist you can make it even though you're hoping they'll tell you not to come.

10. When you're angry, you:

    a. Make sure everybody knows how you feel.

    b. Experience your anger in your body before you do anything else.

    c. Try to think of something else.

    d. Look for a way to get even.

11. To figure out whether you're really in love, you:

    a. Check out how the rest of your life is going.

    b. Spend as much time alone with the person as you can.

    c. Compare notes with your friends.

    d. Assume it has to be love when the sex is this good.

12. You feel it's the last straw when someone cuts in front of you at the supermarket checkout, so you:

    a. Complain to the store manager.

    b. Stand there and fume.

    c. Yell at the guilty party and then cringe as everyone stares at you.

    d. Feel angry and politely let the person know you were there first.

13. You swore you'd never give your irresponsible sister money again, but now she's in tears on the phone, so you:
    a. Refuse, because it's a matter of principle.
    b. Give in, because you know she won't stop crying until you do.
    c. Refuse, because you felt an ache in the pit of your stomach when you started to say yes.
    d. Give in, because you know you'll feel guilty later if you don't.

14. Lord knows you've tried, but you can't seem to warm up to your mother-in-law, so you:
    a. Decide to see her only as often as it feels good to see her.
    b. Rack your brain to find something about her you like.
    c. Think about how you could get her to change her behavior.
    d. Blow off steam by making jokes about her with a sympathetic relative.

15. When you have to make a fast decision, you:
    a. Do a quick survey to get the consensus.
    b. Go with your gut feeling.
    c. Tell everybody they'll just have to wait.
    d. Remind yourself that few decisions are irrevocable.

Personal and interpersonal acumen comes from four emotional skills that make up EQ: emotional awareness, acceptance, active awareness, and empathy. Can you feel strong feelings without dumping them on someone else or numbing them? Can you sustain that accepting awareness in the midst of the chaos we call everyday life, with compassionate understanding of other people's feelings and the aplomb to choose actions that balance your needs with theirs and serve you all? Your answers on this quiz tell you something about your relative strengths in these skills—but only if you've been honest with yourself: Do your answers represent the way you typically act or just the way you believe you *should* act? For many of us, the vestigial instinct to trust our emotions shines through and steers us to the high-EQ answers, even if deep down we know we don't really behave that way. Don't worry if that's true for you. The rest of this book is devoted to helping you bridge the gap between intention and action, which is, after all, what emotional intelligence is all about.

For now, circle or otherwise mark your answers on the charts, then use the charts as a reference along with the following text.

HIGH-EQ ANSWERS

	1	2	3	4	5	6	7	8	9	10	11	12	13	14	15
a						♥	●				●			✳	
b		▼						▼		✳					▼
c	●			♥	♥				●				✳		
d			✳									●			

▼ = High emotional awareness

✳ = High acceptance

● = High active awareness

♥ = High empathy

LOW-EQ ANSWERS

	1	2	3	4	5	6	7	8	9	10	11	12	13	14	15
a	●	▼	✳	✳	♥	○	○	●	✳	✳	○	●	✳	○	▼
b	✳	○	✳	♥	♥	✳	▼	○	♥	○	●	✳	✳	✳	○
c	○	▼	▼	○	○	✳	▼	●	○	▼	✳	●	○	✳	▼
d	▼	♥	○	▼	♥	♥	✳	▼	✳	✳	●	○	✳	♥	♥

▼ = Work hard at chapter 3

✳ = Work hard at chapter 4

● = Work hard at chapter 5

♥ = Work hard at chapter 6

○ = High-EQ answers

People who have an edge in emotional awareness, for example, know that our deep feelings will always win us more votes than any data (2.b), that physical health is crucial to all intelligence (8.b), and that emotional responses are reliable guides to decision making (15.b). If you got these answers right, you may sail through chapter 3.

If you can accept yourself and your feelings, you can accept your own vulnerabilities (3.d). You're not afraid to feel the full brunt of painful feelings because you know they're not meant to last (10.b). You don't let the emotions of loved ones manipulate you (13.c), and you can give without martyring yourself (14.a). Chapter 4, a tough one for most, may be easier for you.

Can you stay on the emotional ball even when you're out in the demanding world? If so, you can maintain your personal integrity even in the midst of charged circumstances without blaming others for their feelings or yours (1.c and 12.d), you know how you feel from minute to minute (7.a), and therefore you recognize your limits (9.c). You also know that it's your whole life that tells you how well any one area is going (11.a). Chapter 5 won't be too difficult for you.

Finally, if you don't presume to know what others need (4.c, 5.c, and 6.a), you can stay aware of others' needs in the middle of your own crises, and you can feel for others without becoming them, you already have a good measure of empathy and will learn chapter 6's lessons well.

Want to know more about your specific emotional skills? Here's how the "wrong" answers break out:

You need to concentrate on chapter 3 if you answered: 1.d, 2.a or c, 3.c, 4.d, 7.b or c, 8.d, 10.c, 15.a or c. Also if it took you a lot more than 90 seconds to complete the aptitude test at the beginning of this chapter, you couldn't remember how you felt about the refrains you listed in "Home Is Where the Heart Is— Or Is It?" and you discovered several afflictions and compulsions in the two quizzes that preceded this one.

You need to work hard on chapter 4 if you answered: 1.b, 3.a or b,, 4.a, 6.b or c, 7.d, 9.a or d, 10.a or d, 11.c, 12.b, 13.a, b, or d, 14.b or c. Also see chapter 4 if the aptitude test showed you're short on humor or self-tolerance, if "Can You Fit In Without Falling Apart?" showed you know how you feel but blame yourself for not conforming, and if other quizzes in this chapter showed you're all too happy to classify and label and you'll go to any length to avoid saying "I feel."

You should focus on chapter 5 if you answered: 1.a, 8.a or c, 11.b or d, 12.a or c. Also see chapter 5 if your "Can You Fit in . . . ?" answers showed inflexibility or poor reflexes, you couldn't click in to your self-recriminations because you weren't even aware of them, or you can't tell what you do in place of saying "I feel" because you can't keep track.

Turn your attention to chapter 6 if you answered: 2.d, 4.b, 5.a, b, or d, 6.d., 9.b, 14.d, 15.d. Also use chapter 6 if you never had any idea what your parents' repeated expressions and gestures meant and the dualism quiz in this chapter indicated you may not categorize things but you feel safer classifying people.

The next four chapters are all centered on a process I call *Building Emotional Muscle,* a progressive meditation focusing on physical sensation. The process starts in chapter 3 and continues through chapter 6 with the aim of helping you acquire all four of these EQ skills. Each chapter contains supporting exercises to show you how to meld your new emotional acumen with your intellect for total intelligence and to help you use that well-rounded intelligence in all those situations where reason failed you in the past. In each chapter I'll give you plenty of benchmarks to measure your progress, as well as a chapter-ending final exam to assess whether you're ready to move on.

How fast you'll progress depends on the strengths you bring with you. Some people graduate in just a couple of months, but most get hooked on EQ and commit themselves to spending the rest of their lives fine-tuning their skills. Just be patient; your initial work will all be internal, so don't expect to become a fully poised citizen of the world overnight.

I hope I've given your intellect all the information you need to act, but I know it's passion that provides the motivation. Let's get started on the passion.

Part 1

FEELING
SMART

3

Welcome to the Elementary School of the Heart

If you're not feeling your emotions below the bridge of your nose, you're not feeling them at all. It's as simple as that.

We often describe emotional events in physical terms—"I felt as light as air," "It was like a kick in the stomach"—but we're only paying lip service to the physical foundation of emotion. When it comes to *feeling* emotion, we let fear and shame warn us off. We've developed some powerful intellectual habits to keep us from following those sensations through to their natural end.

Fortunately, the fact that you're used to thinking and not used to feeling doesn't mean you can't do both. Just as you can rehabilitate an injured arm or leg, you can reclaim emotional awareness from the archives of your personal resources.

The way to do that is by toughening up so you're no longer afraid of emotional pain and loss of control. As I explained in the last chapter, all emotion brings us important information, so it's crucial that you learn to circumvent the fear of feeling. When you get comfortable with being emotionally uncomfortable, you can remember emotionally painful events without being overcome; you can ride out the feelings of the present until the pain is gone and the message has been delivered.

I call that kind of toughness *emotional muscle,* and just like any muscle, it can be built through exercise. Starting in this chapter, I'll give you a progressive exercise for raising EQ called

Building Emotional Muscle. This exercise teaches you to feel your emotions intensely by giving them 100 percent of your attention and using your entire body—not just your heart—to experience them, all in the privacy and safety of your home. Chapters 4 to 6 build on the same techniques, with the ultimate goal of making you so emotionally fit that you can read and identify your own feelings and those of others, no matter how subtle they are, no matter where you are, even when your mind is occupied by a mountain of other tasks.

We'll start out slow and steady. Plan to spend at least a month practicing the Building Emotional Muscle exercise daily and doing the supporting exercises to hone your overall physical awareness and stimulate your body's receptivity to emotional signals. I'll tell you how to gauge your progress and what remedial steps to take if you get stuck. At the end of the chapter you'll find a short final exam you can use to measure whether you're ready to move on to chapter 4.

Here's the basic curriculum:

Elementary School Curriculum:
Emotional Awareness

Every day for 28 consecutive days:

- Practice Building Emotional Muscle, Part I (30–40 minutes).*
- Move—walk, dance, or do more vigorous exercise (pages 70 to 71).
- Wake up to feeling (page 75).
- Use mind joggers to focus on breathing (page 74).

* For every day missed, add 2 days to the 28. For 5 days missed in a row, begin the 28-day cycle again.

Before we get started, let's find out if you feel your feelings below the bridge of your nose. When I ask people at workshops whether they're feeling their emotions physically, most insist, "Of course I feel my feelings in my body. Where else would I feel them?" Most, it turns out, don't have a clue about the kind of physical focus that I'm after because it's not commonly experienced by adults. Have you lost this ability too?

ༀ QUIZ ༁

Feeling Smart: Are You Conscious or Unconscious?

When you're feeling sick, do you immediately know exactly where it hurts? When you're feeling elated, content, or tranquil, can you put your finger on the physical origins of that feeling? Answer the following questions as honestly as you can, and save your answers—you'll need them again later.

1. Where in your body do you feel fear? _____
2. Where in your body do you feel anger? _____
3. Where in your body do you feel joy? _____
4. Where in your body do you feel sorrow? _____
5. Where in your body do you feel love . . .
   for your lover? _____
   for your children? _____
   for your parents? _____
   for your siblings? _____
   for close friends? _____

There's no one right answer for each question, because everyone is unique, but we all tend to feel certain large categories of emotion in the same areas of the body. Fear can be felt as a tension or squeezing in various parts of the body. Anger may be experienced physically as heat or an excess of energy in the stomach, chest, or throat. You might feel sorrow as pain in the chest or heaviness throughout the body; joy as an uplifting, lightened sensation. Naturally, people often feel love around the heart, though the different kinds of love may be felt as a difference in intensity more than physical location.

If you were able to put your finger on any site for most of those emotions, you may be able to move on to chapter 4 in a week or two. But if you couldn't remember the last time you felt any of these emotions at all, or you said you felt any of these emotions anywhere above the nose, you'll definitely have to practice for at least a month and also work hard at the supporting exercises that follow.

I know you'll find the effort worthwhile. You're about to learn aspects of yourself that mental introspection will never reveal and gain a form of self-mastery that eludes the intellect.

· BUILDING EMOTIONAL MUSCLE PART I ·

Building Emotional Muscle is an exercise program designed around the fact that emotional fitness works the same way as physical fitness. You can't run a marathon cold; you can't achieve self-control when you're emotionally numb. You need to rebuild your tolerance for emotional intensity progressively, in part to get your IQ used to sharing control over you with EQ.

When you invite your emotions to surface, your intellect will probably sound the alarm that loss of self-control is imminent. You'll have to expend a lot of active effort to ignore that warning and forge ahead through your fears. In the exercise instructions, I've used words like *allow, release, permit,* and *invite* in a gentle attempt to tell your head to take a backseat and let the feeling experience occur unfettered. But that doesn't mean that you are in any sense passive in this process. You have new skills to learn here, old defenses to dissemble, plateaus to face as well as peaks. You're not some inert receptacle for emotions that are being poured in from the outside. Your emotions come from within you—they *are* you—and it takes courage and sweat to achieve self-control by working through any distress they bring.

Your assignment: Practice Building Emotional Muscle Part I once a day for at least 20 minutes at a time, ideally 30 to 40 minutes, for 28 consecutive days—the time period behavioral psychologists have determined that it takes to instill any enduring change. Plan on spending about a month on each chapter in part 1 of this book, but please think of it as 28 days of consistent effort, because it's always easier to take the process of change one day at a time. You'll build emotional muscle more successfully if you develop body awareness and physical fitness, so also use the ancillary aids under "Muscle for Muscle" that you find helpful.

If you must indulge your intellect, record your reflections in a journal, but don't expect these entries to accurately depict the *experience.* A more suitable use for your mind this month is to let it recognize the changes in your overall well-being, which will result from raising your EQ, and to use the mind joggers on page 74 to support your physical efforts.

Your goal: To be able to focus on an intense feeling for 10 to 12 minutes without being anxious or frightened. Keep in mind, however, that not everyone gets the desired results right away, so don't get discouraged. One workshop participant invested three weeks of diligent effort before he finally began to retrieve his feelings using the exercises in this chapter. Once he did, he described what he had uncovered as "like finding buried treasure." With *daily* practice you'll probably be able to locate and intensify feeling sensations within a week or two. That does not mean that you should try to name the emotions connected to these feelings or determine their cause—remember, this is elementary school.

What to expect from the exercise: In this three-part process you'll begin to empty your mind with tried and true breathing, relaxation, and meditation techniques so you can focus exclusively on physical sensation. You'll put all your energy into following the most intense feeling you discover in your body and you'll then try to hang on to that for at least 10 minutes. Finally, you'll make an abrupt shift from these feelings back to the external world.

What you get will range from numbness to a myriad of physical sensations to full-blown emotional release, maybe including all-out weeping or moaning. Perhaps you'll be baffled by the fact that the anger you're conscious of in the real world dissolves into fear and trembling during the exercise, or that there's distinct pain where you never noticed any before. Don't be afraid; as long as you follow the instructions closely and end the exercise when instructed, you won't be overwhelmed. In fact, you'll discover that you're tougher than you think. When you make the abrupt shift from a pure feeling state to the tangible world around you, you give your mind a chance to register what your body has discovered in the exercise: that you can not only endure emotional experience but emerge from it energized, deeply relaxed, with heightened sensitivity toward yourself, and maybe others too.

Before you begin, read over the following instructions carefully at least two or three times or until you can imagine yourself doing the exercise step by step in the sequence described. You may want to memorize the boxed summary on page 66 to keep yourself on track. You also may want to practice the beginning a couple of times before diving into the middle and end sections—the more relaxed you are, the easier it will be to identify feelings in your body. Give some thought to what you plan to do at the conclusion of the exercise—make a call, wash the car, fix dinner, and so forth.

The Preliminaries
Prepare yourself to build emotional muscle by creating as safe and comfortable an environment as you can:

1. Take off your shoes and loosen your clothing.
2. Take the phone off the hook; lock the door if necessary. You might even wish to hang up a "Do Not Disturb" sign.

3. Sit in a comfortable chair that supports your back, or lie down if you're sure that doing so won't put you to sleep.

4. Set a timer if you have a tendency to keep looking at the clock.

5. Stretch and move around before the exercise to get a head-start on loosening muscular tension.

6. Music may support your use of the process (as it has mine). Music is emotionally evocative. For example, if you've uncovered sadness in one exercise session and want to learn more about that feeling, use music that makes you feel sad. In experimenting with music, I made a tape of classical excerpts that helped me relax and go deeper into emotional intensity. Later, I experimented with other kinds of musical sounds and made tapes using these musical forms.

7. Don't smoke, drink alcohol, or eat during the process. In general, the less reliant you are on drugs or medication the easier it will be for you to focus, because most drugs and medications block emotional centers in the brain.

8. Don't do the process before bedtime. It's crucial that you experience the shift from inward focus, during the exercise, to outward focus immediately afterward. Resuming daytime activities is a much better way to do that than going to sleep.

The Beginning:
Relax and Redirect Your Focus

What to expect: Your body will release and soften. Your shoulders, which are often around your ears, will drop as much as one or two inches and slope downward so that your neck appears longer. Your jaw will release and your mouth open softly. Your fingers and toes will uncurl.

1. Start by tensing, tightening, and then releasing each part of your body from head to toe or toe to head. Focus on each

body part and squeeze for a count of five to seven before releasing it. Do this with the muscles, bones, and visceral tissues in your toes, feet, legs, pelvis, lower back, abdomen, chest, hands, arms, shoulders, neck, head, and face. Let each of these body parts go completely limp, relaxed, once you have squeezed and released them.

2. Clear your mind of all extraneous thoughts. Take several slow, deep breaths, releasing your thoughts with each exhalation. Make sure that you let go of as much air as you inhaled. Put one hand on your chest and the other on your belly. Are both of your hands moving? If not, breathe in a little more fully and let go a little more completely. As you continue, allow your body to sink comfortably into the chair, bed, or floor. You might wish to deepen your breathing by repeating the words "soft belly and soft chest" as you breathe in and out.

It's not easy at first to rid yourself of all your thoughts. It's quite likely, in fact, that they'll intermittently pop back into your consciousness. When that happens, focus on your breathing and again try to let go of those thoughts upon exhaling. You'll probably have to do this now and then throughout the exercise.

The Middle: Focus on Feelings

What to expect: As your breathing deepens, you'll either permit yourself to experience an increase in feeling intensity or fight the process by restricting your breath, falling asleep, or becoming preoccupied by frightening or critical thoughts.

Slowly scan your entire body to determine where you're presently experiencing the most intense feeling. This will be someplace below your forehead, unless you happen to have a headache. Focus all your attention on this one area and *direct your breath to its center.* You may do this by picturing that area as a bull's eye at which you're aiming your breath. Or imagine that it's a balloon that you're going to blow up larger and larger, or a pool that you'll dive into more and more deeply. Experiment with different images from session to session to see which one works best for you.

The most important part of this process is to experience the physical sensations that take place in your body as you breathe deeply into the intensity. Don't be surprised if the first sensation you notice is one of tightness or heaviness—you're tuning in to that logjam of unfelt emotions that this exercise will invite to come out. What many people notice first is a specific pain in some body part.

Allow the feeling you've located to grow by continuing to breathe deeply into the area of greatest intensity in your body. Focus on physical sensations, but also permit yourself to be frightened, angry, or sad if that's how you feel. If you're not experiencing much feeling of any sort, you can focus on what it feels like to feel nothing. You may find it helpful to intensify your experience by repeating "I allow the feeling" on each inhalation and exhalation, as long as you can do so without turning this into a mental demand. You'll know your intellect has intruded if the feeling you're trying to focus on diminishes rather than intensifies.

✍ *Don't push for a release; a bit at a time is just as effective and less frightening. The point here is to allow, rather than force, the feelings to emerge.*

This process is about allowing, trusting your body to tell you how much it wants you to feel or know about in this moment. You'll get better at that over time.

You may begin with one feeling but find that it shifts or dissolves into another, or the source of the feeling may move to another area of your body. That's fine; follow the new feeling as long as the feeling becomes more intense. If it does not, concentrate on your breathing to point you in the direction of greatest intensity.

You may be vaguely aware of a whole slew of different feelings simultaneously. Maybe you notice a generalized ache or squeezing in a large area of your body—like the whole torso. We're complex creatures, and in the real world we rarely feel only one emotion or physical sensation at a time. (Remember feeling a combination of joy and sadness at a wedding, for example?) So it's only natural that a cacophony of feelings might try to push themselves into your consciousness during this exercise. That's fine—your goal is to narrow your focus to the most intense feeling, so keep breathing into the area to see if it shrinks. If not, just focus on the whole area this time out.

Stay with the most intense feeling for 10 to 20 minutes or for as long as you can. Feeling, like a bucking, rearing horse, is full of fear and unbridled energy. The only way to tame it is to *stay with it*. If you discover you're too fearful to focus intensely for more than two to five minutes at a time, that's fine. You'll make faster progress, however, if you can repeat the process two or three times a day, instead of just once, until you can comfortably focus on your intense feelings for at least 10 minutes.

People may cry in this part of the process—not necessarily because they're sad, but often because they've been holding in feelings for so long that it's such a relief to let go. Tears are not necessary for a release to take place, though. Sometimes people moan or make other sounds during the process, and sometimes they stretch or spontaneously move parts of their bodies.

Trembling is a common physical manifestation of resistance—your mind may be saying that this intense feeling is not OK, and you want to remind yourself that it *is*. If you begin to tremble, just continue to breathe deeply and hold your focus on the intense feeling.

If you feel little or nothing, keep in mind that even not feeling is a feeling—it just doesn't have a name. Focus on the experience of nonfeeling, emptiness, or nothingness, exactly as you would an emotion. You probably won't be able to localize the experience, but that's all right. Just treat the generalized experience as you would any other, breathing into it and allowing it to intensify.

The End: Switching Back to the Real World

*What to expect: If you're crying hard, you may be tempted to go on releasing beyond the time you set aside for the exercise—**don't do it**. You can keep on slowly releasing even though you've stopped crying. Redirect your focus and go back to your outer life in the world. You've gone into your feelings so you can come out—not stay in.*

1. When the time you've set aside is over, get up, open your eyes wide, and stretch. Stamp your feet, walk around, and wash your face if you've been crying.

✍♥ Stop focusing exclusively on your feelings and redirect your thoughts and attention toward your normal daily activities.

2. Though your focus has shifted from your inner world to the outer world, you'll retain some of the feeling awareness you recently experienced. Allow the feeling sensations to stay in your body, even though you'll be directing your attention elsewhere.

Taking Stock

You've now completed one exercise session. How do you feel? No matter what discoveries you may or may not have made, you're likely to emerge from the process feeling at once tranquil and energized, ready to return to your daily tasks with renewed vigor and concentration. It's not that different from the way you feel after exercise but deeper and probably without the increased heart rate—somewhat euphoric, perhaps more at peace with yourself than you usually feel. Again, your body will retain a certain level of feeling awareness even though you've shifted your consciousness focus. That's great, and now it's perfectly fine—desirable, in fact—to let your mind do some of the work. It's your body that will feel the beneficial results of the exercise, but you need that rational mind to describe them and to remind you of them so you'll be motivated to keep up the good work. Here are some of the questions your sense of reason may have raised:

What if I didn't feel anything? Just keep at it—repeat the exercise as instructed until you *do* feel something—remember, it took one person three weeks, and he found it well worth the wait. If you're impatient and unwilling to stick with the feeling of not feeling, try this alternative the next time you do the exercise:

1. Before you scan your body for feelings, take a moment to re-create an emotionally charged event in your mind's eye. In other words, self-trigger a recent emotional memory—something not overly intense until you're familiar and comfortable with the process. Perhaps you became uncomfortable in some seemingly unthreatening situation or laughed inappropriately for an unknown reason. Re-create this moment as vividly as you can. Touch, taste, and smell the event as well as hear and see it in your mind's eye.

2. Once you catch hold of a feeling memory, however, shift your awareness to the feeling sensations in your body. DON'T STAY IN YOUR HEAD. Later on, this technique will help you learn to manage more intense emotional memories, but for now keep the recall on the lighter side—until you're familiar with the process.

If after a month of practice, you're still not able to sustain any feeling at all for 10 minutes, add the antifear mantra in chapter 4 to your daily regimen.

What does getting a headache mean? You're not allowing the intensity of a feeling to deepen sufficiently. Perhaps you're holding your breath. You don't have to push for a full release, but there has to be some release. The next time out, remember to return to deep, full breathing whenever the feeling you're focusing on diminishes in intensity or just stays relatively mild.

Can I tell by where I feel a feeling what it means? Exactly where a particular feeling settles has a lot to do with how you contracted your body in an attempt to circumvent emotion as a child. As I said earlier in this chapter, certain generalizations can be made about where we feel certain emotions, but it's too early to worry about putting names to the feelings you've unearthed and certainly too early to try to trace their cause.

You may have noticed that for the most part I used the word *feelings* in the exercise instructions rather than *emotions*. That's because what's important for now is the physical sensation. If the feeling you focused on in the middle of the exercise was accompanied by profound recognition of a certain emotion, that's fine. But if you've had a long history of emotional numbness, what you're most likely to be able to evoke at first—if anything—is unfamiliar physical sensation.

Don't let events and scenes that intrude on your feeling consciousness fool you into believing that you not only know what emotions you've evoked but exactly what caused them. You probably haven't developed enough emotional muscle to assume that this is trustworthy feeling-based information; it's much more likely to be your intellect interfering. Use the benchmark of sustained intensity to indicate whether you've reached your goal for this chapter, and take the final exam at the end before you jump ahead.

How long will it take me? Dyed-in-the-wool intellectuals probably will need the full 28 consecutive days of practice. Others will need only a week or two. Stay in this chapter as long as it takes you to be able to sustain an intense feeling for 10 minutes, and don't cheat. Even 28 days is usually enough only to integrate the process. You can move on to chapter 4 after that period, but it takes most people two or three months to feel comfortable, familiar, and trusting of the process. So keep it up!

BUILDING EMOTIONAL MUSCLE EXERCISE: A SUMMARY

1. Create an environment of comfort and safety.
2. Clear your mind and concentrate on breathing fully and deeply.
3. Relax your body.
4. Take time to scan your body, noting various physical and emotional sensations and determining where you most intensely experience feeling. If your experience is that of being numb, concentrate on the experience of feeling numb.
5. Allow your feelings to intensify by continuing to breath deeply and directing your breath to the area of strongest feeling in your body. Stay out of your head and you will remain in control of yourself.
6. Focus in this way for 5 or 10 minutes, building to 20 minutes—2 or 3 minutes if you do the process 2 or 3 times during the day.
7. End the exercise by shifting your focus from your physical feeling to your daily responsibilities and activities.

I know that's asking a lot. Despite the benefits you'll notice from doing the exercise, it's not easy to keep it up as required. It's hard work, it takes time, it's inconvenient, and we don't always want to know what we find out in the process. So here's a little extra incentive to keep you going . . .

A Brief Pep Rally

How many times have you seen a child on the playground wailing with pain and anguish over a fall, acting as if in mortal agony—and three minutes later running off to play again as if nothing had happened? Children who have not yet been taught to devalue emotion demonstrate that going fully into our feelings *allows us to come back out.* Studies of children demonstrate how readily this birthright can be reclaimed:

• According to Jerome Kagan, eminent Harvard developmental psychologist, though some children are behaviorally inhibited at birth they can change as a result of "emboldening experiences"—processes that stretch EQ by building tolerance of emotional discomfort. By gradually encountering emotional hurdles, shy, quiet, and fearful children master feelings of fear and of being overwhelmed.

• In a Duke university study, one of the key skills for helping older children control angry behavior was found to be teaching them how to monitor their feelings. Becoming aware of their bodies' sensations, such as flushing or muscle tensing, as they were getting angry helped these children stop and consider what to do next, rather than automatically striking out. Even when we've learned inappropriate patterns of behavior, we can alter those patterns by paying attention to feeling experience.

• In adults as in teenagers, depression is often the result of replacing gut-level feelings with repetitive, self-defeating intellectual messages. In two separate studies, learning basic emotional skills enabled teenagers to reverse pessimistic habits of thought that triggered depression.

• Failure to tell one feeling from another was found to be a key factor leading to eating disorders in a group of more than 900 teenage girls. The less skilled they were at managing their emotions, the more serious their disorders were. The same applies to children with addiction problems. Current scientific theory posits that teenage alcohol and drug dependence results from an attempt to soothe feelings of anxiety, anger, or depression.

If you *do* pursue this birthright by building emotional muscle, you stand to enhance your performance in areas where we use emotional awareness or a similar capacity:

• *Your sixth sense.* Emotional awareness is an unassailable— yet unnameable—sense of deep personal truth, a sixth sense of sorts. It's a lightning-quick gut reaction to a given situation; we often call it *instinct*. Building emotional muscle helps you hone the instinct that makes you sense danger even when external conditions seem normal.

• *The flow state.* If you've ever made an effortless perfect serve in tennis or surprised yourself with an artistic creation, you've experienced the flow state, a feeling that comes from deep inside without mental interference. Your racquet or paintbrush seems to become an extension of your arm, and you don't have to think about what to do. Your ability to enter and sustain the flow state is enhanced by emotional awareness—and so are your athletic skills and creativity.

• *The social mind.* To anyone else one cry from a baby sounds the same as any other, but a parent inexplicably knows the difference between a cry that means "I'd like something to eat" and one that means "Help me! I'm hurt!" It's your body, not your head, that tells you the difference. If you don't believe me, try to describe the difference between the two cries in words. The body has a mind of its own, and it's a social mind. Emotional awareness informs us of not only our own feelings but those of others as well. It helps us form incredibly strong bonds with those we care about.

• *Motivation and perseverance.* Building emotional muscle teaches you that pain is not an end but a passage. When you know that pain is constructive and self-limited, you're not too likely to let fear stand in the way of achieving your goals.

All these incentives help many people stick with the task of building emotional muscle. So does the following support.

Muscle for Muscle: Exercises to Support Emotional Muscle Building

I'll say it again: Emotion is a physically palpable experience. So you shouldn't expect to feel emotion fully with an unfit body, any more than you would expect to play Chopin on an untuned piano. Emotional awareness of the variety of human feelings, like a composition using a variety of musical lines, some more prominent than others, creates the texture of our emotional experience. If you're to hear the whole symphony, you have to be able to feel sensation in your whole body.

Unfortunately, many of us still believe we're feeling emotion in the body as we should because we all hear messages that seem to come directly from the heart. Real emotional intelligence requires that we tune in to the emotional chords played by the whole body, from the back of the neck to the tips of the toes.

There are two ways to achieve this: shifting our consciousness back toward the body using various techniques such as mnemonic devices and visualization, and stimulating physical feeling by doing what the body is meant to do: move.

If you didn't feel much during the Building Emotional Muscle exercise, first look to your overall comfort with your physical self. How did you do on the Feeling Smart Quiz at the beginning of the chapter? How conscious are you of your body from moment to moment? Are you unable to answer when someone asks where you got that bruise on your leg? Are you the last to know when you're coming down with something? Can you describe where you have birthmarks and how your body has changed over the years (without flinching)? Do you take the car to go to a store a block away? All the exercises in this section can help you restore your connection between self and body and thus heighten your efforts to regain emotional awareness.

A wealth of evidence tells us that exercise is critical not only to our physical health but also to our emotional and intellectual well-being. Years ago, working with mind brain researcher Dr. Jean Houston, I learned of the direct relationship between random movement and brain cell growth. I learned that all kinds of movement in general, and random movement in particular, sharpen memory and improve IQ. Some creative aging centers have done remarkable work restoring memory and even reversing senility through programs that teach the aged to begin moving again.

I believe that the benefits to EQ from exercise are as great or greater—especially if the emotions that Building Emotional Muscle unveil are distressing ones. Movement and exercise, by stimulating the production of endorphins, the body's natural mood elevators, demonstrate that feeling has the potential for being a joyful process and thus bolster your motivation to keep building emotional muscle.

Inching Along

If you've avoided physical activity or have taken a long hiatus from it, you might find it hard to begin getting regular exercise. One way of easing into a new activity is to pair it with something that you already enjoy doing. Here are some suggestions:

1. Exercise with a friend. Walk briskly, run, bicycle, swim, take a yoga class, or work out at the gym with someone else. (By "someone" I mean a person who will share and thus reinforce the experience, not TV, which is absorbing enough to distract you from your body and cause you to injure yourself.)

2. Experiment with a variety of physical activities, including those that are aerobic, those that strengthen muscles, and those that tone and stretch.

3. Listen to invigorating, inspirational music while you exercise. Music speaks to the body in unique ways. Dance to it, do yoga, aerobics, or calisthenics with whatever kind of music excites and delights you.

As your strength increases, the process itself will become its own reward, and you'll look forward to regular exercise routines. To begin with, however, you might want to ease into movement by choosing one of the two following ways to start your day.

Moving to the Beat in the Morning

By putting you in a positive feeling frame, early-morning exercise combined with music starts you off on the right emotional foot. So if the idea of exercise per se turns you off, why not wake up to a private dance session? Choose whatever music compels you to move and spend 15 minutes dancing. Whether you do it alone or with a partner, from a stately waltz to a rousing jazz routine, it will get your heart pumping and do your spirit good. Let the sound play you, energize you, move you forward—preferably into doing the Building Emotional Muscle exercise!

Cleaning Out the Cobwebs in Your Mind

As an alternative, go for a sunrise or early-morning walk. If a good night's sleep has left some mental litter uneradicated, this simple solution is sure to wipe the slate clean and get you off to a good start every day.

As you walk briskly along, breathe in the colors, sounds, smells, sights, and tastes that surround you. Become these sights, sounds, colors, tastes, and smells. Your body has provided you with some great tools in the form of your five senses. They only get sharper with use, as does that sixth sense we call emotional awareness.

What do you notice that you haven't noticed before? How do you feel during your walk—at the beginning, the middle, and the end?

A daily walk or dance may unlock the emotions that are still hiding when you practice building emotional muscle. If emotional intensity still eludes you after you've been doing this for a week, try doing the emotional muscle exercise directly following your walk or dance. If you don't begin to experience more intense emotion than before, here's some remedial work you can do.

A Few Physical Aids to Jump-Start Awareness

LEARNING HOW TO BREATHE—AGAIN

Breathing is something we all do automatically, isn't it? We breathe, all right, but not necessarily the way we should. As we saw in chapter 2, most of us became shallow breathers in our attempt to limit the flow of oxygen into our bodies. This life-altering practice distances us from emotional awareness.

Put a healthy baby between your two hands and what do you experience? You feel *both* of your hands moving—quite a lot! Your hands will contract and expand two or three inches back and forth as if you were playing an accordion.

Full deep breathing will make you more aware of visceral sensations, and it is the first thing you should concentrate on if you're not getting very far with exercise. The relationship between breath and movement is obvious—activity forces us to breathe deeply. In addition, the flow of blood makes you more conscious of your body.

The purpose of this exercise is to help you reverse a lifetime of shallow breathing. If you tend to fall asleep when relaxed, sit in a straight-backed chair and practice at a time of day when you're normally most alert. Lying in front of a mirror may make it easier for you to be aware of how much your chest and belly are moving. If you're not likely to fall asleep, the exercise may be done sitting, lying down, or walking slowly. Suit yourself.

Make yourself comfortable (but again, not so comfortable that you're likely to fall asleep).

1. Place one hand on your chest and the other hand on your belly and begin taking a series of slow, deep breaths. Hold your breath for a second or two before releasing it, making sure you release all of the oxygen you inhaled. If you don't exhale all of the air you take in, you may hyperventilate and become light-headed—not a serious problem but potentially unpleasant.

To avoid holding in any air, try to push out a little more air after you finish exhaling. You can also count as you draw your breath in and out—perhaps five counts on the inhalation and seven counts on the exhalation. If the breath is full and deep, the process will both relax and enliven you.

As you take a breath, your chest and stomach should expand or lift. Either your chest or your stomach may be the first to rise, or the two may lift simultaneously. It really doesn't matter, as long as there is movement in each area. If there isn't, just keep up the practice of trying to breathe deeply enough to fill both cavities. Within a week or two, you'll notice an improvement, if you continue to practice daily.

2. Once you've established a smooth deep rhythm, imagine that as you exhale air is leaving your body first through your feet, then your legs, pelvis, back, fingers, arms, shoulders, neck, head, and face. The entire process should take 10 or 20 minutes at the most.

3. After completing the exercise, walk around the room and notice how breathing fully and deeply has affected the way you see, hear, feel, and experience yourself. Notice that colors have become brighter, sounds clearer, and feeling more intense. That heightened perception should appear in your practice with Building Emotional Muscle as well.

ACT LIKE A TWO-YEAR-OLD

Still feeling a bit stiff, even with the benefit of deep breathing? You're probably conscious of only about 25 percent of your body. Here's a way to stimulate and get to know the other 75 percent.

Have you ever watched a two-year-old move? If so, you may have noticed that the child's body doesn't move in unison. One part moves in one direction, other parts move in different directions, and the child never repeats the same movement over and over again as we adults do.

Try to move randomly for even a minute or two and see how stimulating it is. When I ask groups of people to move randomly, most of them fall into their chairs exhausted and breathing hard after three minutes, because this type of movement gets the heart pumping and the blood circulating instantly. (I don't recommend this exercise for those with heart problems.) It also shows people how unfamiliar they are with various parts of their bodies. What do you discover when you move this way? That you can move your legs easily but not your head or hips? That you can swing your arms but your lower body feels stiff and awkward? Before you do your early-morning dance or walk or engage in more structured exercise, act like a two-year-old for three minutes. Within a week or two it should make you more aware of those little-used body parts and make your body your own again.

MIND JOGGERS

Staying connected to an intention for change is no easy matter, so an attention-grabbing reminder can be extremely useful. It takes only a fraction of a second to notice and comply:

1. On each of about a half-dozen self-sticking notes, write a word or short phrase that brings to mind what you intend to do: "Breathe," "Breathe fully and deeply," or "Chest/Belly"; "Get up and move" or "Put on some music"; "Practice Building Emotional Muscle today"—whatever captures your attention and reminds you of what you want to accomplish. (Never remind yourself of what you do *not* want to do.) Put the notes in places that you'll see and touch frequently throughout the day—telephones, refrigerators, computers, rearview mirrors, toilets, briefcases.

2. Use moments in your daily ritual to jog your mind. For example, take a moment to check your breathing or your physical vitality before meals or every time you comb your hair or brush your teeth.

WAKING UP TO FEELING

To get used to reflexively assessing how you feel without superimposing thought on the experience, every morning, quickly ask yourself, "How do I feel?" the minute the alarm goes off—before you open your eyes or sit up, if possible. Breathe deeply and do a quick survey of all the parts of your body. Doing this every morning programs you to hold on to your feelings without having to jump into your head as quickly as you're used to doing. To reinforce your effort, try visualization: Before you go to sleep at night, involve as many of your senses as you can in picturing yourself waking up aware of what you feel and able to sustain that feeling before you begin to start thinking. To find out if this exercise is effective for you, also do the next exercise.

POLICING YOUR THOUGHTS

In chapter 2 I asked you to use a clicker to keep track of how often your head jumps into your daily routine with self-recriminations. Now you're going to take this one step further. Use the clicker again to log how often you're able to revert to feelings—saying to yourself, "I should be feeling this instead of thinking about it," when you catch yourself thinking self-critically.

Final Exam: Are You Ready for High School?

If you're ready to move on, you should now be experiencing more of your body, and your range of feeling sensitivity should be growing:

1. Are you more palpably aware of feeling sensations throughout your body? In this moment, can you feel sensations in your feet, inner thighs, shoulders, mouth, throat, inner arm?

2. Can you differentiate between sensations above and below your heart as well as in the area of your heart or above and below your stomach as well as in your stomach?

3. Has the number of times you click for the "Policing Your Thoughts" exercise generally been increasing over the month?

✍ *You're ready to move on when you can say yes to at least two of the preceding questions.*

4. Once you've completed your 28 consecutive days of Building Emotional Muscle, take the Feeling Smart Quiz at the beginning of the chapter again. How do your answers differ from those the first time you took the quiz?

✍ *If your answers are now more detailed, and you reported feeling certain emotions in parts of your body away from the heart or stomach, you're ready to move on.*

Moving On . . .

A little emotional muscle makes us all a lot stronger. By now I bet you've noticed that your energy level is higher, those nagging little aches and pains are starting to fade, and, just maybe, you're feeling a little more at ease in your world. After all, you're beginning to release some pent-up pain, and when you feel better you're a lot more pleasant to be around.

You're beginning to feel a new, improved form of self-control, and you're delving more and more deeply into emotional experience. You know you can take it physically—but can you accept what your emotions say about you? "Ouch," you exclaim, "I didn't know I was that scared!" "Hold it," you admonish yourself, "getting that angry just isn't right." At some point you're going to begin to translate physical sensation into strong identifiable feelings. Many of us treat them the way we'd treat our dog after he's chewed his way through our neighbor's prized Aubusson rug: We'd like to disown them. In the next chapter I'll tell you how to resist the urge to give your feelings away. I'd bet your dog is worth keeping. I know your emotions are.

4

Accepting What You Feel

Q: What do you do with a feeling you'd like to give away?

A: Embrace it.

If you've done the work assigned in the previous chapter, you're probably hearing some inner voices telling you to drop your intensified emotions like a hot potato. *Don't do it.* Attaining emotional awareness and then rejecting what you discover is like following a workout at the gym with a double cheeseburger and a cigarette. Your progress will be halted well before self-knowledge and interpersonal poise become yours.

Two consequences are inevitable if you drop that hot potato: (1) By cutting off your emotions prematurely, you prevent yourself from learning what they are, when they originated, and what evoked them. (2) Because they're not entirely expended, you'll have to find a way to dispose of those feelings, and 9 times out of 10 you'll choose shame or blame, the twin bogeymen of a low EQ.

People who can't accept their emotions—and thus themselves—often seek someone to blame for their anger and convince themselves that their sadness and anxiety are shameful. This not only wastes time and energy but also dulls the senses that we all need to remain emotionally alert out in the real world, where distractions come at us from all directions. Without full acceptance of our emotions, we lose the wisdom to make the right decisions, the driving force behind our passion to act.

Rest assured that acceptance does not mean passive resignation. It does not mean living with pain, allowing yourself to be pushed around by someone else's feelings, or putting up with whatever people do. It means lovingly embracing every one of your feelings (even fear, the feeling that stands in the way of feeling!) as informative in the moment and integral to your being. It means understanding that your emotions are fully bearable, no matter how distasteful they may seem, no matter how strong they get. It means beginning to comprehend that if you can love yourself in this way, you can love others too.

Acceptance is a difficult sticking point for many of us. With elementary school behind you, your body has plenty of evidence that intense feelings can be endured and therefore need not be rejected. But each person's mind seems to have a saturation point for emotional intensity. When you reach yours by turning up the heat in Part II of the Building Emotional Muscle exercise, the mind will do everything in its power to call things to a halt. Maybe you'll find yourself progressing very slowly, in fits and starts. Maybe your intellect will allow you to explore one emotion but keep you from feeling out another. Many people find they periodically need an acceptance refresher course; fear and self-denigration are so thoroughly inculcated that acceptance is the first thing to go when defenses are down for any reason.

That's why you need to bring all your weapons—physical, emotional, *and* mental—to bear in this chapter. To keep your work with the Building Emotional Muscle exercise fruitful, I'll give you exercises for replacing unaccepting mental messages with self-affirming ones. Although you won't yet have the muscle to sustain emotional awareness anytime, anywhere (that's the goal for chapter 5), now and then emotions that you've come to know in the exercise will announce themselves out in the world. I'll tell you how to grab those opportunities to reinforce the acceptability of your emotions. If you persevere, in about a month you should feel accepting enough of your emotions and yourself to know you're ready to venture into the world with your valuable new emotional skills. Here's the plan for learning emotional acceptance:

High School Curriculum: Emotional Acceptance

Every day for 28 days:

- Practice Building Emotional Muscle, Part II (30–40 minutes, plus about 20 minutes for grounding before and after).*
- Continue the exercise program you began in chapter 3.
- Practice the antifear mantra whenever you have a moment— in the grocery checkout, at a stoplight, and so on.
- Use the "Inching into the Real World" suggestions at every opportunity.

As needed:

- Use the "Mind and Body Joggers" and "Waking Up to Feeling" exercises whenever you're dissatisfied with your progress with Building Emotional Muscle.
- Do the humor exercises at the beginning of the month, as directed.

* Add 2 days for every day missed; if you miss 5 days in a row, start the 28-day cycle again.

How Emotionally Accepting Are You?

When you refuse to accept your feelings, they tend to pile up in the amygdala (the limbic structure that functions as the brain's emotional authority) just as they would if you weren't feeling them at all, leaving you with emotional memories that could stuff a landfill. But where numbed feelings may nag at you with health problems from migraines to ulcers, partially felt emotions are likely to show up in chronic emotional responses or behavioral patterns. If you're sad all the time but rarely get mad, or if you're usually angry instead of sad, you're probably trying to cut off another feeling underneath.

As to behavior, the most common indication of lack of acceptance is repetitious activity, from smoking and drinking to excessive TV watching or socializing. We all know that tobacco, alcohol, and drugs are bad for our health, so if you're indulging in these habits I bet you're already aware that you're trying to avoid something. These habits are almost always adopted to numb emotion. It's not as easy to spot the harm in repetitious activities that are generally healthful in moderation, but if you're doing anything to excess, the odds are that you're trying to distract yourself from your feelings. As I'll show in chapter 5, the best way to judge whether any behavior is good for you is to look at how it's serving your overall well-being. Are you waking up exhausted from falling asleep in front of the TV every night? Are you prone to stress injuries because you're heading for the gym whenever you feel irritable, frustrated, angry, or depressed? These are good indications that you're rejecting felt emotions.

In fact any repetitious behavior should be suspect, from biting your nails when you're nervous to an inability to be still. Can you take a walk without a personal stereo blaring in your ears? Can you tolerate gaps in conversation, or must you fill the space between two people with chatter? Do you avoid staying home alone, and when you have to, do you stay on the phone or keep music or TV going all the time? Again, these are all signs that you're feeling emotion but can't accept it. Here's a self-observation exercise for exploring your degree of acceptance more deeply.

✑ QUIZ ✑

Watching the Picture Show Inside Your Head

Can you accept your thoughts, let alone your feelings? Let's find out.

1. Are you aware of the scenarios or daydreams you replay in your mind's eye again and again? For a few days, observe the scenarios you create—the plots, discussions, situations, interactions between people that you love and hate—as if you were watching a series of short-subject films.

2. Does it make you feel comfortable or uncomfortable to realize that you create these scenarios?

3. Would you feel comfortable or uncomfortable telling others about your repeated fantasies? Would you rather die than let anyone know? Would you tell your spouse, minister, kids, sister, best friend, coworkers?

4. Can you begin to identify the feelings triggered by daydreams as needs or longings? Would you feel comfortable sharing the motivations behind your fantasies with the people in your life?

Superwoman fantasies are about power and probably indicate that you don't feel in control and want to be more assertive. Lots of daydreams about romance may indicate that you feel lonely or unfulfilled—not that you aren't loved, but that you may not be able to let that love in. The biggest revelation from this exercise may in fact be that you can't even stay with the so-called positive feelings in your experience. Can you bear to stay with feelings of excitement, sexiness, hope, and love for more than a few minutes at a time? Can you make it a point to really enjoy and intensify a feeling by breathing fully and deeply into it, or do you hold your breath, get something to eat, smoke a cigarette, or mentally play down the event? The reward of emotional acceptance is higher highs, along with more intense lows.

Our most difficult feelings, when experienced halfway, end up distorted by thought and perpetuated far beyond their useful life. Anger, for example, frequently metamorphoses into blame. To spot intellectualized anger, repeat the Clicking in to Self-Scolding exercise from chapter 2, but click in every time you send a "you" message: "You always/never . . ." "You should/shouldn't . . ." etc. More than a couple of clicks a day means you're having difficulty accepting your anger.

Similarly, unexperienced sadness and anxiety tend to show up in your life as shame: "I shouldn't be depressed when so many people are worse off" ". . . when everyone's counting on me to feel cheerful," ". . . because I might die if I let myself feel this way for long." "Only weaklings get this scared." "I'm such a *wimp*—I promised myself I wouldn't get so nervous about this!"

You can spot intellectualized sadness or fear by repeating the clicker exercise or just checking the results you got the first time around. Again, more than a couple of self-blaming, shaming clicks a day means you're not accepting feelings of sadness or anxiety.

Blame and shame turn our fears into self-fulfilling prophecies. A simple traffic jam becomes an accident scene; an uncomfortable social situation makes your ulcer flare. Laying blame over a lifetime leads to a heartbreaking cycle of disappointment and failure. One woman I know divorced her husband because she was sure he was at fault for her constant anxiety. With emotional acceptance she realized her feelings were exaggerated by emotional memories; they weren't shameful and didn't need to be dumped. She went back to her husband on bended knee, and they're together to this day. Others aren't so lucky. Even after a second or third divorce they fail to realize that their spouse is not to blame—their feelings reside within themselves and their own history.

People who gain acceptance by building additional emotional muscle are actually empowered by the discovery that our feelings are ours alone. We can feel in control in the most out-of-control settings when we know that we own something—our emotions—that no one can take away from us. In his book *In Search of Meaning,* Victor Frankl eloquently described how "a life of inner riches and spiritual freedom" helped Auschwitz prisoners "of a less hardy makeup . . . survive camp life better than did those of a robust nature." For Frankl the key to surviving long years of forced labor lay in focusing on feelings of love for his wife, experiencing her presence constantly, rather than on his surroundings.

Such a profound feeling of self-assurance doesn't come cheap—the work gets more challenging and the homework load grows in high school. Let's get started.

· BUILDING EMOTIONAL MUSCLE PART II ·

Time to turn up the heat. Part II of the exercise will help you learn to bear intense feelings triggered by either present events or the flooding of emotional memories from the past. Our most difficult feelings, especially those that are chronic, absorb energy at an unconscious level. Emotional acceptance reverses this process and adds an abundance of energy to our lives. Every time you do this process you'll feel an influx of energy.

Your assignment: To spend 30 to 40 minutes on Part II every day for 28 days.

Your goal: Part II of this exercise should enable you to allow any feeling to intensify. You should be able to focus exclusively on welcome and unwelcome emotions for 12 to 20 minutes, and strong feelings should remain in your consciousness as background even when you're no longer focusing on them. By the end of this chapter you should reflexively breathe deeply whenever you experience strong emotions.

Focusing on emotional sticking points no matter how hard your mind tries to divert you, so you can discover what those sensations mean and how long they've been around, creates positive new emotional memories to counterbalance the negative ones. These new emotional memories make you more accepting of all your feelings.

What to expect from Part II: Part II is still very much an interior process, but one that increasingly stretches beyond the 30 to 40 minutes that you've been devoting to ritualized practice. Consciousness of what you're feeling, especially if those feelings are strong, will pop into focus more and more often. Every time this happens you register an intellectual response (I accept or don't accept what's happening) that will promote or undermine this process.

Before we begin, here's a way to fend off fear by establishing self-assurance.

Grounding the Exercise

If you're even a little fearful of emotions that may arise during the process, you'll feel safer if you ground yourself before and after, through physical movement and exercise or contact with nature and the earth. This step adds about 20 minutes to your exercise session, bringing the total time to 50 to 60 minutes.

1. Before you begin the process, take a vigorous walk, turn on some music, and dance or exercise. You can also ground yourself by making contact with the earth. Take a walk in the woods or dig in the garden.

2. Do similar things at the end of the exercise. If you're crying, stand up, open your eyes wide, stamp your feet, walk briskly around. Move vigorously, dig in the garden, or go for a walk.

3. Practice the exercise at a time of day when you feel rested.

The Beginning

Start just as you did in chapter 3—relaxing, clearing your mind, and breathing. Now, however, you should be able to achieve relaxation and deep, full breathing more easily.

The Middle

Continue breathing into the center of the feeling, allowing it to grow in intensity.

☛ Start out slowly if you need to and add a minute or two each day. The point is to stretch your tolerance for experiencing emotional intensity just a little each time you do the process.

Focus in this way for at least 5 and up to 10 minutes, then deepen the experience by posing the following questions to the place in your body that feels most noticeable or most intense—heavy, dense, warm, or tingly. The questions are to be flashed across the screen of your mind, not pondered. If nothing happens when you flash a question, move on. The idea is to maintain your focus on feeling.

Are you a new feeling?

If not, how old are you? When did I first experience you?

Do I experience you often or just occasionally?

What is the nature of this feeling?

- Is it sadness or hurt? And if I am sad, what makes me sad and why?
- Is it anger, frustration, or rage? If so, what makes me angry and why?
- Is it fear? If I'm afraid, what makes me fearful and why?
- Is it gladness, joy, or enthusiasm? Again, why?
- Is it caring, tenderness, or love? Again, why?

Let whatever answers come be OK. And if no answer comes, let that be OK, too! Don't dwell intellectually on insights that may occur. Instead, sustain your focus on physical feeling until you end the exercise.

Tears may flow; you may groan, cry out, speak, or wail—but not necessarily. Progress at a very deep level can take place quietly.

The End

After focusing in this way for up to 20 minutes, stop! Again, ending is very important because it is essential that you experience a shift from a feeling focus back to an intellectual focus.

Don't spend more than one hour total from beginning to end. The point is to take this tool out into the world and use it there.

Practice consistently until you're comfortable with any emotion that may be triggered in you. Be patient and gentle with yourself—the more frightening the feeling, the longer it will take you to grow comfortably accepting of its role in your life.

What if I start shaking uncontrollably? Breathe, breathe, breathe! The shaking has to do with anxiety, and there's nothing to be afraid of. Open your eyes if that makes you more comfortable, take very deep breaths and walk around, but don't stop focusing. It's OK to shake—nothing bad will happen to you as long as you continue to focus within your body and breathe deeply. (This of course assumes that you don't have a physical condition that might account for the shaking and may need attention.) Also remember that you don't have to focus for more than two or three minutes at a time. Take it slowly. Working with intense feelings that you're having a hard time accepting may slow you down, and you may have to take it a few minutes at a time again. That's fine.

Are you sure this isn't indulging in emotion? Remember, you're going in for the purpose of coming out. Like an infant who must bond first with the mother to become an independent, self-reliant individual, you surrender to emotional experience in one moment to free yourself of the influence of an overly excited amygdala. Every time you do the process it brings about a little more tolerance for emotional intensity and a little more self-control and releases a little more energy.

How can I tell when I've become genuinely accepting of myself? The litmus test for emotional acceptance is your ability to take a flood of emotional memories in stride—when you can remain tolerant, forgiving, calm, and accepting of all your intense feelings. When strong emotion no longer frightens or limits you, you know the deeper meaning of acceptance.

How long does it take for a strong feeling to run its course? In doing Part II some people uncover very strong feelings, and even though the intensity diminishes when they redirect their focus from inner to outer experience, they continue to feel the emotions' presence. However, I've never known a feeling to maintain a strong presence for more than 36 hours—after that the intensity diminishes rapidly. In any event, you'll know the process is working for you because you'll think and work with an increase in energy—provided you follow the instructions.

A Brief Pep Rally

Everyone feels the grip of fear during Part II of this exercise. To cultivate an internal environment of emotional acceptance you have to come to grips with that fear. Strong feelings are likely to take you into the realm of the unknown and bring you face to face with your fear of losing control. Powerful fear-based anxieties are often hidden under emotions like hurt or anger.

When you feel chronically hurt, sad, angry, or ashamed and allow these emotions to build or deepen, what you'll uncover is fear. We see this in the fact that not everyone we come into contact with can hurt us or make us mad. Only people who have some power over us—who can pose a threat to us—upset us. If a child or a drunk says something nasty, most people will hardly notice. If the child is ours or the drunk someone we count as important, and the remark poses a threat we take seriously, we may have a feeling reaction. Perhaps the implication in what we hear is that we are not good enough, not likable or lovable. This in turn can spark fear that we may lose our job or our status, or have to face rejection. When we dig a little under our feelings and ask why we're angry or hurt, we eventually get to an answer that speaks to one or more of our many fear-based memories or beliefs.

This is not to say that fear is a bad emotion, only that it is self-defeating to numb or intellectualize fear. Anxiety, fear that something bad *may* happen, is at the core of many of our self-defeating responses.

We also know that we can feel overwhelmed with fear in situations that are obviously not life-threatening at all. When we feel emotionally overwhelmed in contexts that pose no danger, the amygdala in our emotional brain has triggered a storehouse of emotional memories. Something has happened that reminds us of a threatening event in the past, and our amygdala floods us with those frightening memories.

Because fear is often a hidden emotion, its staying power is strong. Building Emotional Muscle Part II practiced consistently will in time break down your resistance to accepting your feelings. In the meantime, however, you can persuade your head to stop opposing you by reminding it of the scientific basis of the exercise.

The techniques tapped in Building Emotional Muscle Parts I and II are founded in abilities that children use quite naturally to gain a sense of mastery over painful feelings and the events that caused them. By repeating a frightening, emotionally charged situation again and again in a familiar, safe, controlled setting, children prevent traumatic events from overwhelming them. In his book *Emotional Intelligence,* Daniel Goleman describes how repeating the game Purdy—a reenactment of a mass murder that took place on the playground of a California elementary school in 1989—helped children who were there calm their overwhelming feelings about the event. This is a clear example of how children use play to gain control over their feelings about real life.

This is exactly what we're doing when we practice Building Emotional Muscle. As adults, we too can heal the past and become comfortable with feelings (past and present) by recalling painful, frightening, overwhelming emotions in settings that are structured, safe, and self-regulated. In addition to revealing what we feel, the exercise provides us with new experiences that give us a sense of composure in the face of emotional intensity.

You can pile up positive new emotional experiences even more quickly using a simple technique for countering fear:

ANTIFEAR MANTRA

As a way of coaxing IQ to accept feelings—and in turn supporting your efforts with Building Emotional Muscle—repeat this chant throughout the day, whenever a few seconds are available or an emotion that you're afraid of occurs.

Take a deep breath in as you say to yourself, "When I feel angry," then exhale as you say to yourself, "it's OK," and focus on an image of yourself feeling, looking, and acting OK—whatever image you find both comforting and energizing.

For "angry" substitute ashamed, jealous, envious, fearful, foolish, embarrassed, helpless, dependent, sad, depressed, excited, sexy, loving, hopeful, or in pain. Work with any feeling that you suspect is difficult for you until you can repeat the mantra without experiencing stiffness or tension anywhere in your body.

Taking Stock

You need a lot of new memories to counteract the charged-up old ones and pave a clear path for doing Part II of the exercise, so try to get in the habit of using the mantra regularly early in the month. You'll see the payoffs in the form of these noticeable results:

1. You'll discover that many of your strongest feelings have been around for quite some time. When you shut off your mind during Part II of the exercise, you liberate the body's considerable memory facility. When allowed to zero in on your feelings, your body can easily distinguish the familiar from the unfamiliar, the old from the new. Just as your body remembers how to pedal a bike after twenty years without a bike ride; just as it warns you of disease by recognizing sensations that were never there before, it can tell you whether an emotion has just come up or has been bloated by many years of feeding itself. The stronger the feelings that arise during Part II, the older they probably are. Don't be surprised if your IQ chimes in with memories of its own, confirming your body's conclusions by bringing up the event that first stimulated the feeling.

Knowing that these emotions are antiques helps you accept them as your own—they're not the fault of your husband, your wife, your kids, your boss, your secretary, your dry cleaner, or the supermarket cashier. Being able to distinguish old from new feelings will also guide you to appropriate actions and reactions to events, as you'll learn in chapter 5.

When thirty-eight-year-old Susanne did Part I of the exercise, hoping it would illuminate the cause of a vague feeling of discomfort she'd noticed in the last few years, the sensation that was repeatedly most intense was in between her throat and chest. She described it as a warm buzzing feeling, almost like electricity. The more she repeated the exercise, the more intense the feeling became. This told her that it had been with her for quite some time, and she was eager to learn more.

2. You'll also start identifying the emotions that arise during the exercise. In Part II, you quickly plant mental queries and then let your body give you the right answers. As you ask whether the emotion is anger, sadness, fear, and so forth, notice what happens to the feeling you're exploring. When you hit upon the name for the emotion that you're sensing, you'll immediately feel more energized, you'll feel right on a gut level, and as a result you'll feel as if the intensity of the emotion has lessened. You'll *know* what the feeling is and can then add the association between a particular sensation and a nameable emotion to your physical, emotional, and mental memory banks.

When Susanne asked questions about the electrical feeling she sensed during the exercise, her energy increased when she hit the answer that it was anger, and she was able to focus more deeply. Each time she repeated the process in this way the emotion's hold on her diminished. Similarly, when she asked about the feeling's age and cause, she eventually discovered that it had been around since her divorce ten years ago. That certainty was confirmed when she found herself occasionally noticing the same feeling whenever her new lover seemed distant, and she noticed that it always tripped an urge to say "*You always* back off when I want to talk about something important to me."

3. You'll discover that no matter how strong they are, you can bear your emotions. Segueing smoothly from the intense feeling of Part II to the mundane demands of everyday life will prove it to you—and in the process start offsetting those nasty emotional memories with pleasant ones. These new memories give you the fortitude to feel out your informative feelings in the real world. Thanks to her work with Part II, Susanne knows she can endure her anger and that it's not her new lover's fault. She has vowed to take a deep breath the next time she feels the sensation.

Inching into the Real World: Techniques for Becoming Accepting Away from Home

One significant result of practicing Part II is that you'll begin to be conscious of some of the emotions the exercise has revealed out in the real world—intermittently, most likely when an event evokes intense versions of those feelings. Take a deep breath, relax, and use your head to take note of what caused the feeling, how it resembles one you've been exploring in the exercise, and that it doesn't need to hurt you in real life any more than it hurt you in the exercise. All this will happen almost instantaneously because our minds are so quick, and that may give you time to stop the reflex actions that fear encourages.

Sharon, whose defensiveness had become legend among her coworkers, used Part I of the exercise to discover that her stomachaches were usually a sign of anger or fear. But she was still having trouble cutting off her angry retorts at the office—she never noticed the knot in her belly until the damage had been done. After putting a few weeks into working on Part II,

Sharon reported this coup: "Last week a woman I've started to get friendly with came up to my desk and said she couldn't have lunch with me because she had to go home and feed her dog during lunch hour. Well, I knew she was making excuses and was about to tell her I had better things to do too, when suddenly I felt this twisting throb right under my navel. I *stopped*—for the first time I can remember, I didn't say anything I'd regret!"

You'll need chapter 5's lessons to govern your actions using EQ all the time, but for now you can inch into real-world EQ in several ways:

1. Be on guard for your emotion-fearing mental habits; they will always return with a vengeance when fear based on lack of acceptance comes up. Do you find yourself trying harder than ever to impress people with how smart you are? Do you find yourself needing to make a pat comment or quote an authority? When that happens, do some extra work with Part II and pay increased attention to the supporting exercises that follow.

2. In chapter 3 you learned to notice how you feel when you wake up. Past efforts to ignore discomfort that you woke up with usually meant that starting out on the wrong foot was bound to ruin your whole day. Now when you recognize some nagging discomfort such as a depressed or irritable sensation, breathe as fully and deeply as you can, focusing on that feeling. Also be sure to exercise—not to distract yourself from the feeling but to sharpen your body's receptivity to it. This technique should ensure that you experience the feeling, possibly discover its cause, and go on to a productive day.

3. Let's say you're at work, shopping, or in any social situation where you're surrounded by other people, and you feel a stab of emotion. If it's immediately followed by a jab of fear (which you now probably recognize from your work with Part II or which you can identify by the impulse to numb the feeling or distract yourself), extend the "Heading Off Fear" exercise from chapter 2. Begin by taking a deep breath and then continue full, deep breathing, relaxing, and focusing (which you should be able to do quickly now) while you ask yourself if you recognize the feeling and how old it is. If it helps, use the focal point image that works for you in the exercise to stay with the feeling. If you can, go to the bathroom or your car, lock the door, and do the exercise, even if you have only two minutes for it. You can also repeat the antifear mantra on page 90.

4. Use your real-world experiences to remind you how harmless your emotions are out there. Every evening, find a quiet few minutes to review the emotional events of your day and the consequences of having experienced your feelings. Did you show your irritation to your boss when you got angry? Nothing terrible happened as a result, did it? Did you focus on your sadness over a tragedy without losing your mental concentration? Compile these positive memories every day to remind yourself of the efficacy of experiencing your feelings whenever they occur.

5. The best way to avoid blaming others is to experience the raw sensations of anger rather than succumbing to the temptation to intellectualize. Building Emotional Muscle can help you do that. But we all have a history of intellectualized anger, so we're all prone to laying blame. To counteract it cognitively and take responsibility for your own feelings, zero in on those "you" messages you send—the ones you kept track of earlier in this chapter. Now whenever you hear yourself starting to deliver a "you" message, try substituting "I." This will feel forced at first, requiring you to shift mental gears that have become pretty rusty. Susanne, for example, has to come up with a fast "I" substitute for "You always back off when I want to talk about something important to me." How about "I feel discounted when you don't want to talk" or "I get the feeling you don't want to talk to me. Why not?" "You" messages are conversation stoppers; "I" messages bring fruitful dialogue.

6. Also pay attention to your "busywork" responses in various situations. If your usual response to a perceived emotional threat is to chatter, attack, go on the defensive, or engage in numbing habits, you know your goal should be to stop yourself. If your typical reaction is to become paralyzed or run away, stand firm. If you can't do that yet, don't be disappointed; you'll concentrate on translating accepting awareness into action in chapter 5. For now you can support your efforts in Building Emotional Muscle Part II by doing the following exercises.

Using Your Head and Your Humor to Fight Fear: Exercises to Support Emotional Muscle Building Part II

You're driving down the freeway, late for your 9:00 A.M. meeting, when traffic comes to a dead halt. There's no way you'll get there by nine—or even before the meeting is over.

Typical reaction before emotional acceptance: You pound on the wheel, scream, swear at every other driver, tailgate . . . you may even cause an accident.

Typical reaction after emotional acceptance: You pound on the wheel, scream, swear at every other driver, maybe even tailgate . . . but only for about two minutes, after which you get a glimpse of your purple-faced wild-eyed self in the rearview mirror and collapse in laughter. You pull over to the safety lane to compose yourself before you hurt someone.

Pushing past the sticking point of emotional intensity to learn acceptance is incredibly challenging, albeit vastly rewarding, work. You'll be relieved to know that laughter is a cornerstone of your high school curriculum. That's because humor and acceptance feed each other in a perfect symbiotic relationship. By interrupting fearful thoughts, humor helps us be more accepting. The reverse is also true: Acceptance makes it easier to laugh at our foibles. We're more compassionate, more forgiving when we laugh.

Humor, in fact, represents the ideal amalgam of IQ and EQ. Reason helps us recognize absurdity when we see it, and a good belly laugh or uncontrollable fit of giggles is one of the most instantly recognizable physical sensations signaling emotion. Laughter brings us into our bodies. Humor cuts through anxiety, grounding us in endorphin highs that lift the heart. In the midst of painful and frightening events and situations humor gives us sweet respite—time to recharge and refresh.

The research about positive feelings that Norman Cousins compiled and popularized made it clear that humor can even make the difference between life and death. I won't ask you to test that theory at this stage of your education, but I will ask you to approach the exercises and quizzes in this section with a sense of fun and a willingness to laugh at yourself.

All of us are natural comedians; we constantly do things that are contradictory, ridiculous, and genuinely funny. I, for example, work at appearing elegant and glamorous but never fail to drop a big gob of whatever I'm eating on the front of my silk blouse. Comedy and humor begin at home, so start with yourself. Look for the contradictory, ridiculous, and funny things you do all the time. Note the discrepancy between what you intend to do and what you actually do, the funny mistakes you make, the indelicate things you inadvertently do, and do your best to laugh at the lot.

Take time out to enjoy funny and absurd parts of life and human nature. Go to a playground and watch children interacting—look familiar? Attend your next cocktail party with a view to human nature. Spend time observing yourself and others in almost any setting and you're sure to find plenty of humorous material. Noticing how widespread likable buffoonery is can help you embrace your own emotions and foibles in a loving, accepting way.

APPRECIATING THE EMOTIONAL PRATFALL: LEARNING TO LAUGH AT YOURSELF

Laughter says, "I'm imperfect, and that's OK with me. I don't need to be other than exactly what I am, and if that's a soft touch, a stuffed shirt, a klutz, or a slob, so be it." Here's a tough assignment: Design a comedians' roast for yourself. To do it well, you have to find out what's truly funny about you:

1. What part of the country are you from? Comedians make fun of regional quirks all the time, and each of us has them. Can you learn to mimic your own accent or dialect?

2. Make an audiotape or a videotape of yourself, preferably while you're with friends so you can see how you act with others. Better yet, ask a family member to turn on the video recorder without your knowledge to catch you candidly. Then view or listen to the tape. We all cringe the first time we hear our recorded voice or watch our expressions and gestures. Breathe deeply and forge ahead, taking notes about your most irritating traits to use in the roast.

3. Pluck up your courage and choose one immediate family member, one close friend, and one coworker to interview about what that person finds funny about you. Take notes for the roast.

4. Now write your roast and record yourself reading your routine. Listen to or watch the tape once a day for a week or two and whenever you're feeling sour. You should find yourself getting at least a few chuckles out of it even if you're no comic genius. For extra credit, revise it as you go along whenever a funnier idea comes to you. For extra extra credit, play the tape for a friend.

THE REPORTER FROM MARS

As you did in the clicker exercise in chapter 2, spend a few days—up to a week—observing your habits of judgment, criticism, blame, and shame. Only this time around create an imaginary visitor from Mars and bring him, her, or it along for the ride. The reporter from Mars has no idea of what is OK, good or bad, right or wrong, wise or stupid, and so forth, in human terms. Each time you catch yourself being critical, stop and ask what the reporter from Mars thinks of the situation. The reporter's viewpoint is especially refreshing when it comes to matters that embarrass or shame you.

Does the whole idea of this exercise strike you as unbearably silly? If so, consider this assignment a priority. Serious intelligence is impossible when you take yourself too seriously. The reporter from Mars views you the way we all view Chaplin's Little Tramp in the classic movie of the same name—as flawed, silly, yet quite lovable. When you can laugh at yourself, everybody else finds your foibles charming, too. Acceptance of ourselves is infectious.

Can you look at yourself with the same loving acceptance as the reporter looks at you, as you view the Little Tramp? Can you hold on to the spirit evoked by this exercise once it's over? The closer you get to replying with an unqualified yes, the closer you are to self-acceptance.

Final Exam: Are You Prepared for College?

By now you've amassed a lot of felt experience, so trust your heart and gut to answer these questions honestly:

Repeat the chapter 2 clicker exercise for a couple of days.
1. Are you less self-critical than you used to be? Do you have fewer opportunities to click in than you did at the beginning of this chapter or in chapter 2?
2. Are you less worried or afraid of others judging or criticizing you than in the past?
3. Are you less afraid of getting angry or feeling sad than you used to be?
4. Are your natural highs higher?
5. Do you find yourself laughing increasingly at things that you used to take very seriously?

ℒ♥ *You're ready to move on when you can answer yes to question 1 and to two of the other questions.*

🖤 *If you can see positive change in yourself in 4 out of these 7 scenarios, you're ready to move on.*

• When was the last time you had a cold? A headache? If you're getting minor ailments, aches, and pains less often than you used to, you may already be gaining some acceptance. A growing sense of better health is one of the first signs many people notice.

• Are you leaping out of bed these days instead of creeping out? Just as doing the Building Emotional Muscle exercise leaves many people invigorated, learning acceptance often increases your overall energy level.

• How do you view exercise these days? No longer a chore but something to look forward to? That's a sign that you're becoming accepting of your body, just a short hop away from accepting your feelings.

• What kind of feedback are you getting at work? If your performance at whatever you do seems a little bit better, it may be thanks to acceptance. A lot of mental energy is wasted on self-castigation over feelings; freeing up that energy leaves us all a little sharper.

• How many times have you snapped at someone today? Long checkout lines, stalled traffic, red tape, and rudeness irritate us all, but when we accept our feelings they don't build to a steady state of irritability. If you're acquiring acceptance, daily hassles may not bug you as much as they used to. Occasionally you find yourself able to follow the dictum, "Don't sweat the small stuff."

• Do you find yourself chastising yourself less often? Are your internal dialogues fewer and farther between? Can you laugh at your mistakes? Emotional acceptance and self-acceptance go hand in hand.

• Are you feeling more patient and tolerant of other people's imperfections? Self-acceptance is a springboard to empathy for others.

Moving On . . .

Give yourself a hearty pat on the back if you've determined you're ready for college. Acceptance is a huge emotional hurdle to make. Fortunately, it brings proportionately great rewards. Accepting your feelings thoroughly enough to stay aware of them out in the world gives you the benefit of vastly increased intelligence for wise decision making and interpersonal poise. I know you're eager to get going, so let me show you how to translate feeling plus thought into action.

5

Living in the Moment:
Active Emotional Awareness

I know you're dying to find out what you'll gain when you flex your hard-earned emotional muscle out in the world. And if you've done the work required in chapters 3 to 4, the moment you've been waiting for is here.

It's time to act!

You now have at your disposal the stalwart informants of your heartfelt intentions: You can feel all your emotions, no matter how strong. In this chapter I'm going to tell you how to take that ability along wherever you go, so you'll always know what's important to you. All you need to turn intention into action is one more layer of muscle. I call it *active awareness,* and it's simply a matter of refining the skills you already have and molding them into lifelong habits so you can call on your emotions to enlighten you anywhere, anytime.

You'll keep your body sensitive and fit so it stays receptive to emotional messages even when you're not at your best and life is at its distracting worst. You'll welcome the full spectrum of informative, motivating emotions so that every day you learn something new about yourself and take another step toward self-fulfillment. And as your mind keeps track of how much headway you're making with your emotions and your body, you'll be gaining intelligence that's greater than the sum of its parts.

That's feeling smart, and it's all the motivation you'll need to adopt active awareness as a lifetime habit. I won't need to remind you that the payoffs are incalculable. You'll see the rewards for yourself. Will you make lots of subtle adjustments so your current life fits like a custom-tailored suit . . . or meet a stranger inside and take yourself off on a brand-new adventure? It all depends on what you want from life. All I can promise is that you'll gain the power to use everything you are and everything that happens to you to shape something of value for yourself and others.

EQ 101 in this college curriculum is more phys ed. The only way to stay linked to your emotions when you're going about your daily business is to keep your body constantly aware of them in the background—and that takes acute sensitivity. The final part of the Building Emotional Muscle exercise will give you perfect emotional pitch.

I'll also give you a couple of mind joggers to support your new habit, but the crux of the curriculum is something of a work/study program. I want you to get out there in the halls of life and learn by doing: Stay attuned to your feelings in the background, and whenever an emotion seems relatively strong or prolonged, use the intensifying technique you learned in Building Emotional Muscle Parts I and II to bring it into quick focus and see what it reveals.

I guarantee that you'll do this more and more automatically as time goes on. Throughout this chapter I'll show you how other people have used the three functions of active awareness—rapid-fire emotional feedback, sustained passion, and a long-term monitor of well-being—to make accurate, intuitive decisions, to remain active participants in their own destiny, to develop emotional self-control, and to hear their own voices amid the voices of others. These examples will outline how a better relationship with yourself translates as better relationships with others. How you fill in the self-portrait is up to you.

College Curriculum: Active Awareness

Every day for 28 days:

- Practice Building Emotional Muscle, Part III (7–15 minutes).*
- Make sure you're noticing an increasing range of emotions in the background and bringing some emotion into full focus (100 percent attention) several times a day as you go about your daily business.
- Use the mind joggers in this chapter.
- Continue the exercise program you began in chapter 3.

* Add 2 days for every day missed; if you miss 5 days in a row, start the 28-day cycle again.

For the rest of your life:

- Use all your resources—emotional, physical, and mental—to increase your self-knowledge and improve your relationships.
- Keep your emotional instrument finely tuned by sticking to good exercise, diet, and rest habits, including keeping a food diary.
- Be on the lookout for signs of emotional disconnection.
- Take remedial action as needed.

Step One into the World: Reaching Active Awareness Through Physical Sensitivity

It's the subtle sensations, not the punch-in-the-stomach and heart-swelling feelings, that help us negotiate the gray areas of life. Some things will always feel wrong to almost everyone— really hurting ourselves, destroying another person or anything of beauty or value—but we live our lives mostly in those gray areas. Gut-wrenching, heart-rending feelings alert you to a major problem, but the little pings and twinges may be telling you that you should have spoken to your client personally rather than leaving a voice mail message, or that you feel a little empty at the end of the day because your rushed evening routine allows too little time with the kids. Heeding these lesser signals motivates you to make the small changes that head off bigger or chronic problems.

Unless you've become an astute listener, however, you won't hear subtle emotional messages when other matters are vying for your attention, as they always do. You need to practice until constant awareness of emotional cues becomes second nature. You're already well on your way. How many emotional messages are you hearing now?

❧ QUIZ ❧

Are You Actively Aware Now?

Where do you *often* notice feeling?

1. In your genitals?
2. In your chest?
3. In your stomach?
4. In your intestines?
5. In your lower back?
6. In your upper back?
7. At the back or crown of your head?
8. In your neck?
9. In your shoulders?
10. In your hands?
11. In your feet?
12. In your toes?
13. In your calves?
14. In your inner thighs?
15. In your underarms?

16. In your wrists?
17. In your ankles?
18. Around your mouth?
19. Around your nose?
20. Around your eyes?
21. In your jaw?

At this point you're most likely to be conscious of feelings in the areas near the top or middle of the list. Just about everyone can easily detect genital and visceral feelings, where we have lots of nerve endings. By now you may also notice feelings in the parts of your body you used to numb your emotions earlier in life. If you clamped your lips together to avoid experiencing anger, strained your eyes to avoid crying, or repeatedly cracked your knuckles when anxious, you may eventually notice that you feel those emotions around your mouth, eyes, or hands. To form the habit of active awareness you need to make sure you can feel sensations in the other body areas on the list as well.

Here's the key method for making sure your body remains sensitive to all feelings, great and small, throughout the day.

• BUILDING EMOTIONAL MUSCLE PART III •

The purpose of the third and final part of this exercise is to make the consciousness with which you end the process a steady part of your life. Active awareness is the ability to stay attuned to your feelings in the background at all times and to shift instantaneously to 100 percent focus on a feeling on command. *Once you have already learned Building Emotional Muscle Parts I and II,* the best way to learn that skill is to sharpen your perception of the most subtle physical feelings.

Your assignment: Practice the exercise for 7 to 15 minutes a day for 28 consecutive days.

Your goal: To be able to feel *something*—even if it seems intangible and is difficult to describe—in every part of your body. When you can do that, you'll notice everything from vague sensations to the physical manifestations of any old feelings you've adamantly refused to feel.

What to expect from the exercise: Because of your practice with Parts I and II, you'll immediately feel sensations in some parts of your body. Other areas, though, may take much longer to awaken. It isn't essential that you *immediately* experience feeling in every part of your body. Take your time and keep pursuing whole-body awareness as your eventual objective.

The Exercise

1. Relax and breathe deeply as you're used to doing at the beginning of the exercise.

2. Focus for a few seconds on the following parts of your body, allowing the intensity to grow as you imagine yourself breathing, penetrating, and intensifying your awareness of these areas: genitals, heart, stomach, intestines, lower back, upper back, neck, shoulders, hands, feet, inner and outer thighs, arms, wrists, ankles, the area around your mouth, jaw, and the back or crown of your head.

3. Now, rather than focus on one part or another in particular, hold on to that overall feeling state for two to five minutes. See and feel yourself staying attuned throughout the day. A small piece of your attention may still be with each of the parts you focused on, but as awareness fans out to encompass or include many points, each point becomes less intense. Taken together, all of the points you focused on represent a felt consciousness whose presence can continue to be felt even though you are not paying strict attention to it.

If by the end of the 28-day cycle you can't identify *some* feeling in most parts of your body you've focused on, continue practicing. How far you pursue the goal of experiencing feeling throughout your body is up to you. Extremely painful feelings that have been numbed may block sensation in some area for a long time. Again, take your time. Your body won't let you go where you aren't ready to go. Just remember that the more you feel, the more aware you will become.

Meanwhile, complete two work/study assignments during the month:

1. Make a point of noticing the range of feelings that hums along in the background of your consciousness during your daily routine. It should be broadening and deepening, bringing new event–emotional response associations to your attention all the time. Take stock at the end of the day; review what you've learned about yourself.

2. Make sure you're bringing at least one or two emotions into the foreground during the day at first—more later in the month. Just use the Building Emotional Muscle process that you now know so well—breathe, relax, focus—to instantly turn 100 percent of your attention to the feeling. Then, just as quickly, let it go and return your attention to the outer world as you did at the end of the exercise.

As time goes on the active awareness background-to-foreground, attunement-to-focus shift becomes automatic. You won't have to pause between attunement and focus or between thinking and feeling any more than you pause between moving your left foot forward and then your right. You'll notice you can function productively and creatively and yet remain conscious of such things as how tired you are or how much pleasure you derive from an experience. Toward the end of this month this boon should materialize as increased efficiency and concentration.

You should feel increasingly energized and motivated to act on your intentions. Your overall experience should be gradually becoming richer, more complex, with more subtleties. You're learning to live in the richness of the moment rather than the stale past or the unformed future.

Learning to Live in the Moment

When you're training your body for active awareness, you'll notice two benefits almost immediately. Both keep you anchored in the present, and consequently both create a framework for effective action.

Is This What I Feel Now or What I Felt Then?

First, you have the power to distinguish between a purely in-the-moment feeling and one compounded by emotional memory. An emotion created by the mind or evoked by emotional memory comes on in a flash, out of nowhere. One minute you're calm and in control; the next minute you're biting someone's head off for a minor offense or running like a scared rabbit, never looking back to see that no real threat exists.

That's how Hilary felt when someone cut in front of her in a department store cashier line during the holidays. When her gut instantly filled with burning heat, Hilary took a deep breath into her chest and belly, then brought that feeling of anger into full focus. Immediately she recognized an old feeling she had explored in Building Emotional Muscle Part II. At the same time, Hilary's IQ informed her that she was paralyzed by her rage and that her head was already swimming with blaming epithets toward the hapless soul who had cut in front of her. All of this information—physical, emotional, mental—told Hilary that this feeling was disproportionate to its trigger and that current irritation was being exacerbated by anger from the past.

Her response? She continued to breathe deeply into the feeling until it subsided and she could say without peevishness, "Excuse me, but I was here first." This entire episode lasted about 30 seconds.

When similar incidents and feelings kept coming up, Hilary did what you too should do whenever feelings that are disproportionate to current events trouble you regularly: Use Building Emotional Muscle Part II (see Chapter 4 for details) to familiarize yourself with the feeling and the past events that you associate with it.

✒ Each time you do the process with a particular feeling its intensity will decrease, and each experience will feel less overwhelming than the next. This means you're gaining control over the emotional charge connected to emotional memory, and each experience will feel less overwhelming than the next.

Refining your body's sensitivity will also make you aware of recurring physical feelings connected to emotional memory. Do you take aspirin for a stiff neck after stressful meetings? Do your legs feel heavy and clumsy at certain times of day or with certain people? Building Emotional Muscle Part II might reveal that as a child you always tensed your neck muscles when with your exacting grandmother or smothered your sadness over your parents' divorce through compulsively active play. Practicing the exercise will not only decrease the feeling's intensity but add to your knowledge of what triggers your anxiety or sadness. When you're ill, dealing with emotional trauma, or taken by surprise by a long forgotten emotional memory, awareness of those triggers will help you avoid them and the extra emotional stress they bring. Fortunately, active awareness also gives you a way to gauge whether you are already under stress due to lack of overall well-being.

Is This the Right Thing for Me?
Second, when you stay in touch with subtle sensations in your body, you know what your energy level is, you know whether you're thinking clearly, and you know whether you're feeling positive toward other people. Bring that heavy feeling in your legs into focus, for example, and you may unearth nagging exhaustion. Pull that feeling of having cotton between the ears into the foreground and it will crystallize as a lack of mental

clarity. And that itch somewhere between your stomach and chest? It could be generalized resentment of those around you. *Pay attention to it.* Energy, mental clarity, and positive regard for others are the three most important benchmarks of well-being. If any one of them is missing, you may be on the wrong course.

When you're *consistently* aware of *all three* of those gauges of well-being, you can always follow the path that makes you feel most energetic, sharpest, and most connected to others. And if you can't *tell* where your energy level, mental clarity, and positive regard for others stand, *consider it a red alert that you've disconnected emotionally.*

There are times in life when everyone lets active awareness slip—or has it wrenched away by a traumatic crisis. When you disconnect from your feelings, you lose not only the information they supply but also a lot of the emotional muscle you've built. You'll spare yourself a lot of heartache if you catch disconnection and take remedial action quickly. Take the following quiz as a self-check when you're stressed by illness or an emotional crisis or when you notice a growing sense of dissatisfaction with your life.

ᴥ QUIZ ᴥ

Recognizing Disconnection

1. Can you tell what's going on with your energy, clarity of mind, and feelings for others? If not, you can be sure you've disconnected.

2. Have you lost control emotionally? Do you find yourself having temper tantrums? Are you ever immobilized by fear or overwhelmed with hopelessness and helplessness?

3. Do you feel victimized? Are you blaming others instead of feeling raw anger to its finish? Are you constantly scolding yourself?

If you answered no to question 1 or yes to questions 2 or 3, you need remedial education:

If you skimped on Building Emotional Muscle Part I, II, or III, complete those assignments now. Acquiring the skill of active awareness depends on devoting the prescribed time to each step of your emotional education.

If you completed the 28-day cycle and feel you achieved a respectable measure of active awareness at one time, do whatever you can to remove yourself from emotionally stressful situations, put off significant decision making or any work that requires mental concentration, and get back to a safe and private environment where you can begin a standard 30- to 40-minute session with Building Emotional Muscle Part II. That single session may reveal some buried emotional memory that's thrown you, and you may be able to reconnect immediately. If not, continue the practice, going back to Part I as well if you can't sustain emotional focus at all, daily until you feel your active awareness return. You can use the final exam at the end of this chapter to gauge whether you have in fact become actively aware again.

Even if you've done the work and are not under any particular stress, your active awareness may be a bit intermittent at first. Don't be discouraged—your head can help.

Mining the Mind: Forming the Awareness Habit

POSTING ACTIVE AWARENESS IN YOUR MEMORY

The mind joggers in chapter 3 can be adapted to help you make active awareness an ongoing part of your life:

1. Write on self-sticking notes anything that catches your attention and reminds you to attune to feeling sensations in your body. Ideas: "Lights on?" "Tuned in?"

2. Put mind joggers in places that you frequent during the day—rearview mirror, refrigerator, computer, bathroom, sink, phone—and keep them around until active awareness feels as natural as breathing.

AT THE SOUND OF THE BELL . . .

This reminder works only where it won't impose on anyone else. (The people around you in a concert hall, at yoga practice, or in your place of worship may not appreciate it.)

Just set your watch to ding at regular intervals—try every hour at first and then move to every two hours, every four, every six. When you hear the ding, ask yourself "How do I feel?" If you can't answer quickly (or at all), keep working at it.

Step Two into the World: Logging Self-Discoveries

The whole point of developing active awareness is to translate your feelings into action. For that your intellect is indispensable. Your mind is the repository for all the event–emotional response connections you make by staying plugged in to your feelings from moment to moment. Once you've achieved emotional sensitivity via Part III of the exercise, your job is to stay *mentally* attuned to the discoveries you're constantly making about yourself and your behavior. When you do, you'll observe those self-motivating payoffs I mentioned at the beginning of this chapter. It works like this:

1. Attunement to your feelings makes you aware of habitual actions and statements that do *not* represent the real you. A pat party line never passes your lips without recognizable discomfort, and what you say and do begins to reflect the true you. You're demonstrating *integrity*.

2. Meanwhile, the intensity or peculiar character of some feelings becomes so familiar that you begin acting reflexively on them. A certain tension in one part of your neck tells you to take a break before responding verbally to someone; a pleasant swelling high in your abdomen says, "Act now—this decision is right." You find yourself wasting a lot less time. You're gaining *efficiency*.

3. You recognize with ease the difference between old feelings springing from emotional memory and new ones that are linked to a current event. You begin to comprehend that you don't have to get angry every time anyone acts imperious or underhanded. You're developing *flexibility*.

4. You've stopped repeating your mistakes, your decisions are sharp and appropriate, you act quickly but "thoughtfully." Your family, friends, and coworkers think so, too, and they say so. This gives you *confidence*.

5. With that confidence you begin to look for ways to take active awareness to its full potential. You continue to take good care of your body, since it's the medium that communicates your emotions. You use your head to reflect on feelings that confuse or surprise you and are gratified to discover that decisions based on them make logical as well as personal sense.

So, to ensure that you're using your feelings to their full benefit, start collecting data on the ways the three functions of active awareness lead you to appropriate action. I can't predict exactly what those will be, so I'll rely on the experiences of other people to illustrate.

1. The Right Place and the Right Time: Acting in the Here and Now

How many times have you felt frozen by indecision when a quick response was crucial, or blurted out words that you regretted but couldn't take back? With habitual active awareness you'll get a constant flow of information, as if from a lab full of discreet but vigilant monitors: Heart rate normal a second ago but now increasing . . . flushed skin, though the room wasn't hot a minute ago . . . squeezing in the chest below the heart . . . neck starting to stiffen . . . "Is that a cramp in my left calf?" Such rapid feedback helps you act appropriately in *this* moment. Here are some of the benefits you should notice and exploit:

Seeing the wisdom in saying or doing nothing. Belinda used to jump in and do the wrong thing out of nervousness in every situation. Now active awareness stops her—"I feel this strange twang, like a plucked guitar string, right above my navel"—and she's learned to do nothing at all until she arrives at a decision that immediately makes her feel energized, mentally clear, and benevolent toward those around her. Bruce used to think that not having an opinion was wishy-washy, so he made sure everyone knew how he felt about any issue—even when he didn't know how he felt. Now he feels sort of fuzzy-headed and tired when he starts to make some bold statement without any emotional conviction. These days he says less and less, and when he is moved to speak he always feels "stronger and surer than ever" afterward.

We're all subject to abundant social pressures to be forceful, active, and productive—or at least to look like we are. When active awareness tells you that what you're about to do isn't right, and no alternative immediately makes you feel energetic, mentally clear, and benevolent, let yourself be silent and still. As time goes on, you'll make fewer and fewer mistakes because you'll be able to resist the strongest pressure to fill gaps with uninformed actions.

Sharpening your reflexes. While you're able to resist the compulsion to act before you're ready, you'll also notice that some decisions come to you instantly. "When it's right, it's right," says Frank. "My staff gave me a list of possible names for a new product last week, and when I hit the right one it was like a brilliant little light went on in my head and my chest. It literally lifted me out of my chair, I was so enthusiastic. I didn't even bother to read the rest of the list." Emotional messages are powerfully motivating, but we've been trained to justify our choices by mentally reviewing all the alternatives. Don't waste your time. A strong emotional signal like the one Frank got should be trusted every time.

Sorting out simultaneous feelings. Barry recognized after a long day at the office that he was hungry, tired, and excited about the next day's trip. A brief focus told him excitement was strongest, so he pushed on; if it had been hunger or fatigue, he would have taken a break. The strongest feeling is often the one that compels us to act or speak, but it's still important to recognize the mix of feelings experienced, because it gives you more options for response. And sometimes intensity is not the ruling criterion. As your active awareness becomes more astute, you'll be moved in many mysterious ways—mentally log all of them.

Adapting to change. If in the past you always felt as if life was passing you by, or you were always "the last to know," chances are you weren't attuned to your emotions, the most reliable barometer of change because they keep you fully conscious of each successive moment. Do you feel crabby in the office today, even though things seem to be going fine for you? Maybe something's afoot in office politics and you need to dig deeper. Does your after-work energy seem to dip lower every day? Time to check your feelings about your home life. If there's a problem, you'll want to do something before it's too late. It's tempting for all of us to fall back on mental rehearsals and fantasies about the future, but if you'll instead tune in to what your body tells you about *this* moment, you'll begin to see the writing on the wall.

Standing firm. Maintaining a strong emotional connection to your needs and values gives you the fortitude to stand up for what you feel is right. "I used to cower and cringe when my boss started her blustering act," recalls Mary. "She seemed so sure of herself. Now that I'm sure of myself, I don't give in so easily. When I feel like I've got the energy for a full-scale crusade, it's full steam ahead."

People who are new to active awareness are often so taken by their newfound strength that they *do* take on the world. But remember that being strong doesn't have to mean acting tough. As your emotional intelligence matures, your feelings will lead you to choices that may not conform to anyone else's expectations or standards; that may even seem inconsistent with your own usual behavior. "I was at a dinner party the other day when an elderly man started making racial jokes," says Gene. "A few months ago I would have thought I had two choices: Do something about it or like it. But this time I realized a third choice was right in this particular case: dislike the behavior without making a stink over it. I didn't *have* to try to change the man, and I didn't have to worry about how my inaction looked to anyone." When a decision *feels* right, it *is* right. Don't think you have to justify it.

2. The Unsevered Connection:
Knowing What You Want Means Going for It

As Carl Jung said, "Emotion is the chief source of all becoming conscious. There can be no transforming of . . . apathy into movement without emotion." Being in touch with your desires is bound to mobilize you into action of some sort, perceptibly and beneficially.

Setting priorities. When you feel torn by external demands, take a minute to focus on your emotions before you plan your day. It took Andy only seconds to discover that his feet felt heavy and his chest hollow because he was remembering his daughter's reaction last night when he'd told her that he'd have to miss her basketball game so he could write his report. How did he know that going to the game turned out to be the right choice? Because doing that left him so energized that he got his report done in half the usual time after the game.

Intern Sharon gave up her volunteer work singing and telling stories to orphans because she feared it would interfere with her studies. But when she decided she hated medicine and wanted to quit, it became clear that she missed what had brought her to medicine to begin with—working with children. When she went back to volunteering, she renewed her love of pediatrics—and stayed at the head of her class.

Grabbing the chances of a lifetime. Tod never cried, but he didn't let himself feel good for long, either. When he met Linda, he kept finding himself wanting to sprint down the block on his walk home from work, but stopped himself because it wasn't dignified. Luckily, he raised his EQ, and when he felt as though he was about to float off his feet, he breathed into the feeling. "I felt like a balloon!" he exclaims now, from the home he and Linda just bought together. "If I hadn't been able to stay with that incredible feeling, I wouldn't have realized that Linda is the love of my life."

Caution, fear, common sense—we have so many reasons for passing up golden opportunities. At the top of the list is our equating feeling good with self-indulgence. Probably much of the work you did in chapters 3 and 4 addressed painful feelings. Now that you're out in society, don't treat pleasant feelings as if they're merely the absence of unpleasant feelings. *Pursue them with equal vigor.*

Making tough decisions. Feelings that flow naturally from choices that build health *persist*. If it's right to seek a divorce, admit a parent to a nursing home, or end a friendship, you'll feel a little better right after making that decision, and any doubts should be erased by the later effects: an increase in energy, focus, and caring for others.

But don't expect a single stab of any emotion to guide you through all the hazards and challenges of life. If your feelings about a problem are strongly conflicting or muddled, give yourself time to sort out the feelings until something turns up dominant. And if you know that the situation is complicated and sensitive, make no move until you're sure you know how you feel about each factor involved.

3. What's Good for Me?
Taking the Pulse of Long-term Well-Being

Active awareness provides a monitor of your physical as well as emotional well-being. You will know when a cold or the flu is coming on and be in a position to take appropriate action. Here are a couple more ways that active awareness keeps you happy and healthy over the long term:

Making life-preserving choices over a lifetime. Market-driven cultures attempt to make decisions for us about what to do, buy, and believe in. Active awareness can help you stay focused on what's right for you in the face of these persuasive pressures—some of which, by the way, will come from people you love and respect. Active awareness also gives you the ability to listen to others with differing views without compromising what *you* need to do. When you're in constant touch with your emotions, you don't need to flit from one self-help program to another in search of salvation. You find it within.

Achieving your long-term goals. Any long-term decision, relationship, or situation can be monitored by using your feelings to gauge your energy level, mental clarity, and positive regard for others. You've got a "great" job but come home totally drained, despite the fact that you love the people you work with and feel creative on the job? Time to look at the job situation—how can you change things to keep what's good for you but avoid being drained of energy?

The whole concept of goals takes on a different meaning when you live in the moment. Each day becomes precious, and your long-term goals become directions rather than fixed destinations: "I need this to feel good, and I'm going to move in this direction," rather than "I'll take step A now, step B tomorrow, and step C the next day—even if it kills me—to be sure I reach point D." The little shorthand rules for how to live our lives that accompany many rigid goals back us into corners that don't speak to who we really are or how we are evolving.

Saying good-bye to self-delusion. So many people fool themselves into believing their course in life is right for them. Such self-deception simply isn't possible with active awareness. Maybe you think you love your lifestyle because everyone else admires it; with active awareness you can't ignore that it doesn't make *you* feel good. Perhaps you'll find out you're not the party animal you thought you were or the loner you believed yourself to be. Possibly your emotions will reveal that you don't like being with the people you thought you liked and you love being with the people you thought you had no interest in. Most important of all, you may find out that the discoveries you made about yourself last year don't hold true this year. Remember that these revelations do not represent mistakes you've made and are nothing to be ashamed of. Instead they are valuable information and should be used as such.

Where are your self-discoveries leading you today? I'm sure you're happier with yourself, and I bet you're also happier with other people.

Step Three into the World:
Connecting to Others by Connecting to Yourself

Contrary to what you may have believed in your pre-EQ days, it's not shutting off your own needs that enables you to respond to the needs of others. Steady-state knowledge of how you feel while living, loving, working, and interacting with others is in fact the key to building and preserving strong and meaningful connections to other people. When you can assert your own needs with calm self-control, rather than with blame or emotional extortion, as you will with active awareness, you relieve other people of responsibility for your feelings and establish an atmosphere of mutual respect.

Bess was at a family gathering when her sister-in-law started to extol the wisdom of holding the family reunion at her house rather than at Bess's, which was "so much smaller." Bess noticed a vague sinking sensation, but her head conveyed nothing but confusion. Immediately switching her feelings to the foreground, she did a quick scan of her body. "It was all in my stomach: a knot in the center—that's always anger in my case; a cold wave— that's fear for sure; and then this smaller bag of rocks that feels like it's hanging from my breastbone—hurt. I almost always notice anger first, so ordinarily I would have spit out a retort. But with this group that's trouble, so I aimed my breath like arrows at all those feelings to see which one seemed most urgent.

Fear was strongest, but hurt was most urgent. Kind of like the difference between volume and frequency. Anger was loudest, but the high frequency of that hurt was impossible to ignore. So I pictured myself wrapping my arms around myself and said calmly, 'My house is large enough, and it means a great deal to me that the family gather there.' To my amazement, no one objected!"

Sid was overcome with embarrassment when he couldn't remember the name of the client in front of him. But instead of running from the banquet room, he took a couple of deep breaths and relaxed while focusing briefly on the feeling. His head cleared, and he remembered that he wasn't stupid—just poor with names. Knowing how he really felt about himself kept him from panicking and restored his self-control. Being able to laugh at himself as he admitted his weakness elicited empathy from his client and put them both at ease.

When you don't have to strain to hear your own voice, you find yourself hearing others with crystal clarity. Bruce is no longer compelled to offer his opinion on everything, because now he's not afraid that listening to others will prevent him from hearing himself. Gene knows that an audible inner voice is all it takes to hold on to one's convictions, so he didn't need to speak out and risk hurting his wife's favorite uncle and possibly his wife to preserve his integrity. Laura would like to get closer to her younger sister, Clara, but where Laura is organized to a fault, Clara is the quintessential free spirit. Clara asked for Laura's help with her taxes, and Laura hit the ceiling when she discovered that Clara's receipts weren't in order. The minute the harsh words were out of her mouth, however, Laura felt the hurt her words had inflicted and apologized.

As your active awareness improves, you, like Laura, will be able to catch such gaffes in midsentence and ultimately before they pass your lips. You'll know how others feel, just as you know how you feel, without using cognitive methods to interpret body language and other cues. With the profoundly powerful tool of active awareness, *you'll feel the messages sent by others in your own body.*

No, it's not always that simple, and I'll explain how you can heighten your receptivity to the emotions of others in chapter 6. For now, you can keep your intellect occupied by registering all that feeling has revealed to you about others and your relationships with them and how this has reinforced the value of developing active awareness to its fullest. How do you really feel in relation to others? How do your actions affect your relationships? How do the behaviors of others affect the way you feel? The swift and authentic answers that active awareness delivers add up to vastly increased social knowledge. When your brain blends your knowledge of what's going on both internally and externally with knowledge of what has happened in the past, you gain intuitive understanding of what's likely to unfold in the future. This intuitive knowledge is the basis of wisdom.

Step Four into the World: Staying Physically Sensitive for Life

Active awareness requires us to make a long-term commitment to all-around physical well-being. I've already made the point that there is an intimate relationship between emotional awareness and exercise. This relationship also extends to our rest and sleep habits and our food choices.

Are you getting enough rest? According to the latest research on sleep by Thomas Wehr of the National Institutes of Mental Health, "Americans kid themselves into thinking that they can get away with five or six hours of sleep." They can, but only if they're willing to function with a disabled IQ. Sleep deficiency also lowers EQ. If you doubt this, ask any parent!

If you've exercised through the elementary and high schools of the heart, you probably have a lot of feeling-based information on the condition of your body. For many of us, though, diet is another matter. We're so accustomed to food-as-recreation, so prone to smothering feelings by eating, that we're much less conscious of how dietary habits affect our overall state of being. The following exercise can be a real eye-opener.

DISCOVERING THE FOOD-FEELING CONNECTION

1. For three days, eat in your usual way. Select the foods and the times for eating that you normally do.

2. Make a chart or log of all that you eat, including in-between nibbles and snacks. Don't kid yourself—you won't remember it all unless you write it down.

3. Pay attention to your feelings, physical and emotional, five minutes after eating, an hour after eating, and two or three hours afterward.

4. Notice any shift or change as the result of eating. Do you feel better or worse than before you ate? Do you feel energized or tired? How well has eating made you feel overall?

Keeping this diary will heighten your awareness of the relationship between what you eat and how you feel even if you *think* you already know the answers. What you record for the first three days will undoubtedly surprise you. Dietary effects can be subtle. You may spot a habit—a certain food, eating at a certain time, and so on—that lowers your awareness. If you're successfully building active awareness, you should also notice at least a few changes in your eating habits over subsequent weeks. If you're more attuned to how caffeine affects you, you may avoid that third cup. If eating a heavy lunch makes you groggy in the afternoon, you might start choosing salads.

We're flooded with advice on health and fitness, of course, and I won't add to the deluge. A commonsense approach is probably best, as always, but my principal advice is to evaluate fitness on a feeling level. How does a particular physical activity affect your energy? What happens to your decision-making ability when you begin exercising or exchange one eating habit for another? How do your fitness choices affect all manner of feelings? From a feeling perspective, fitness takes on a new character.

By now I hope all your resources—mental, emotional, and physical—are working for you, inching you toward self-mastery and self-fulfillment. If you keep up active awareness, you'll never stop growing emotionally. As your self-knowledge grows, you add richness and complexity to your life—something I think of as a fourth dimension. More on that in chapter 11; for now, let's see whether you're ready to learn the skill you need to balance your own needs with those of others.

Final Exam: Have You Learned Active Awareness?

✍ *Don't move on until you can say yes to question 1 and two of the following questions.*

1. Is the range between your intentions and your actions narrowing? How many of the things that you want to do, do you in fact do? Is the gap between "I want to" and "I have" narrowed? How much more often are you able to accomplish what you set out to do, be it acting to improve your health, your relationships with others, or your work?
2. Do you feel more motivated than you used to?
3. Do you feel more energetic than you used to?
4. Do you experience more mental clarity than in the past?
5. Do you feel more autonomous?
6. Do you feel friendlier, more caring, more loving toward yourself and others than you did in the past?

Moving On . . .

The more you learn through your own feelings, the more attuned you become to the feelings of others. I can't think of a more potent tool for navigating the maze of human relationships. It's empathy, and it's the last skill you gain when you educate your heart.

6

Becoming Empathic:
How Intelligence Becomes Wisdom

We're not alone out here.

Of course you knew that, but how do you *feel* about it? If you're feeling pretty fortunate to be a social being these days, you must be making great strides toward habitual active awareness. When you can stay attuned to how you feel all the time, empathy—knowing how others feel—comes naturally. Then it's just a hop and a skip to balancing your needs with others' to everyone's satisfaction. Another small jump, and you're adept at forming enduring, mutually respectful relationships.

Chapter 5 gave you a few glimpses into how seamlessly empathy flows from active awareness. In this chapter I'll show you how to avoid common obstacles to empathy and how to keep your understanding of others growing throughout life.

Why knowledge of our own feelings can make us so fluent in others' emotional language is not entirely clear—to scientists *or* philosophers. Chalk it up to our shared biology and the irresistible pull of one another's company. Whatever the explanation, consider empathy a generous bonus for all the work you've done so far. Constant active awareness makes you feel smart. Empathy makes you feel wise.

Daniel Goleman called empathy "the fundamental people skill" in *Emotional Intelligence.* "People with empathy," Goleman says, "are natural leaders who can express the unspoken collective sentiment and articulate it so as to guide a group toward its goals." As shown in tests with over 7,000 people in the United States and 18 other countries, the benefits of being empathic included being better adjusted emotionally, more popular, more outgoing, and more successful in romance.* According to emotional intelligence researchers Thomas Hatch and Howard Gardner, empathy is the necessary ingredient for charm, social success, even charisma.

If you don't quite fit that profile yet, it's likely that the specter of your low-EQ past is casting a shadow on your brilliant future. In this chapter I'll show you how to use empathy to full advantage by overcoming a nonempathic upbringing, your fear of vulnerability, and any judgmental attitudes. I'll illustrate how you can use empathy to balance your needs with those of others. Finally I'll demonstrate how empathy, when extended to an ever-widening circle of people around you, turns into constructive compassion. With active awareness you have the power to live in a way that's right for you. With empathy you become a citizen of the world.

Postgraduate Curriculum: Becoming Empathic

You don't have much new work to do now, so proceed at your own pace.

- Continue the efforts to enhance your physical sensitivity that you began in chapter 5.
- Use the quizzes in this chapter to determine which obstacles may stand in the way of your taking full advantage of empathy. Then do the accompanying exercises.
- Seek out opportunities to use your empathy in all relationships. Use the "Give and/or Take" exercise to experiment

---

* Daniel Goleman, *Emotional Intelligence* (New York: Bantam, 1995), 97.

with balancing conflicting needs and prepare yourself for Part 2 of this book.
- Explore your boundaries by turning empathy into compassion.

Just like active awareness, your empathy may be intermittent at first—strong with loved ones but spotty with strangers (or vice versa!); sharp in comfortable environments but dull where you're less secure; unfailing when you're fearless but unreliable when you're frightened. The following quiz will tell you how consistently empathic you are.

✒ QUIZ ✒

Testing Your Comfort with Empathy

Take a few minutes to relax and breathe deeply so you can answer the following questions quickly, honestly, and without making judgments.

1. Do you generally feel comfortable at home and secure with other people?
2. Do you like having pets (or wish you had one if you don't)?
3. Do you feel renewed and at peace by a walk in the woods, on the beach, in a meadow?
4. Do you ever notice feelings that contradict what someone is saying—the anger behind a placid expression, the sorrow beneath a modulated voice, the joy behind measured words?
5. Do you always know it right away when something you did unintentionally makes someone else feel bad?
6. Can you let yourself experience the feelings of someone who has been hurt by something you did intentionally and may do again?

7. Can you keep listening even when someone asks for more than you feel comfortable giving?
8. Do you become defensive when someone you care about tells you that you have hurt or disappointed him or her?
9. Can you listen without having to agree or disagree with someone?
10. Do you stop listening to people when you get scared?
11. Can you remember what the other person's complaint was the last time you had a dispute with someone?
12. When your child experiences a major disappointment, must you do something immediately to take away the child's pain?
13. Do you believe you have to shut out the other person's needs to say no?

If you're able to demonstrate empathy in a variety of circumstances, you should have said yes to questions 1, 2, 3, 4, 5, 6, 7, 9, and 11, and no to questions 8, 10, 12, and 13. You can attune to other people's feelings, needs, wants, and desires while remaining fully aware of your own *separate* emotional experience. You can feel another person's pain without giving yourself away or having to control the situation in some way. You derive this power from the same physical, emotional, and mental resources that you call into play in active awareness. In the midst of the most heated argument, for example, you know precisely when to stand firm and when to yield, because you're acutely aware of how you and the other person feel about the point of contention. That facility translates as the ability to achieve a consistent balance between your own needs and those of others—an acrobatic feat worthy of the Wallendas—in love, at home, and at work.

If you didn't do too well on this quiz, it's probably not because you're oblivious to the emotions of those you encounter. If you learned active awareness as you should have in chapter 5, that's not possible. Of course, if you treat pain and suffering as inconsequential laughing matters or you immerse yourself in others' pain to the point where the line between your identity and theirs is blurred, you haven't done the required work. Go back to chapter 5 and keep at it until you can pass the final exam.

Opening Yourself to Empathy

More likely, when you do hear someone else's feelings you sometimes try to shut them out. Are you occasionally overassertive, letting your head veto your body's recognition that an issue may not be worth fighting over because it's just not as important to you as it is to the other guy? Do you find yourself drifting back into the tendency to rehash conversations because what seemed so right for you left you with a vaguely uneasy feeling? Do you leave interactions feeling as if you've missed something that was going on? Maybe your head is at odds with what your body perceives. Let's get them back together.

Getting Over the First Hurdle: A Nonempathic Upbringing

I know of a two-year-old whose mother found her rocking her baby brother's cradle in the middle of the night. When the little girl's mother asked, "What are you doing?" the child answered, "Baby crying."

I know of a six-year-old whose younger sister became deathly afraid of worms after finding half a worm in half an apple she had eaten. On rainy days, the younger child dreaded walking to kindergarten because the rain washed worms onto the sidewalk. On such days the six-year-old carried the five-year-old, almost as large as she, to school and back.

I also know of a three-year-old boy who loved animals and refused to eat meat because, as he put it, "I don't eat my friends."

We're born to be empathic. In fact, experts in developmental psychology consider the inability to experience the feelings of others within the first few years of life a definite cause for concern. Once they've ruled out physiological defects, these scientists will begin to look at how the child has been treated. *That's because children treated with empathy are more likely to treat others with empathy.*

The little girl whose big sister understood her fear of worms knew that; several years later she made it a point to walk from class to class with an obese child cruelly shunned by the other children. Delve into your memory, and I'm sure you'll find evidence of your own.

Did your mother know when you were blue without a word from you? Do you remember your father breaking into a rejuvenating grin when he was bone-tired, because he found your youthful joy contagious? If so, you may be naturally empathic. Or were your fears pooh-poohed; your disappointments demeaned? Did your parents dive in to fix things whenever you were really upset . . . or did your upsets end up distressing them so severely that you ended up comforting *them?* If, for whatever reason, empathy was not an element in your upbringing, the following exercise can strengthen your resolve to stay empathic.

CREATING AN EMPATHIC INNER PARENT

As you prepare for this or any imagery exercise, keep in mind that it's only as powerful as your ability to experience it at a physical level. Thought-driven processes alone are always ineffectual. You have to experience what you're imagining physically and emotionally to impact your deep memory bank and your immune system.

In this exercise you'll implant in your deep memory bank the image of a nurturing inner parent. This parent will hold and touch you lovingly, protect you from harm, set limits for your good, and teach you how to be a loving parent to yourself and others.

1. Begin by carefully planning the image of your inner parent. The parent you construct can be based on a real person or a composite of several people (male and female). You can also borrow from books or films. What you're looking for is someone mature and wise, someone who knows how you feel and loves you unconditionally.

2. Make yourself comfortable in a chair or lie down. Focus on the arm that you usually write with and feel it growing heavier and heavier. Bring three or more of your senses into the process—see, touch, smell, taste, and above all feel what is happening to your arm. Move your focus to the other arm and do the same thing. Feel it grow heavier and heavier. Now shift your attention to the leg that corresponded to the arm you began with. Feel, see, sense this leg growing heavier and heavier. Now do the same thing with the opposite leg.

3. Repeat step 2, only this time suggesting that both your arms and legs are warm.

4. Now concentrate on your breathing and repeat twice: "My breathing is full and easy; my breathing is full and easy. It breathes me."

5. Now center your attention on the area around your heart and repeat: "My heart beats evenly." Focus on the regularity of your heartbeat.

6. Shift attention to your brow and repeat twice: "My forehead is pleasantly cool."

7. Now imagine yourself in an idyllic setting walking alongside a body of water or in the high mountains or in the woods—wherever (in or out of nature) you feel safe and comfortable. Hear the birds singing, feel the warmth of the sun on your body, smell the sweet scents that surround you and enjoy.

8. Once you feel relaxed and safe, introduce your inner parent into this setting.

9. Imagine yourself as an infant or very young child and experience your inner parent lifting you up, holding you tenderly, speaking softly to you, and giving you whatever it is that you need to feel content. All you may want at first is to be held and soothed, but this may change after you've done the exercise for a time. You may also grow in age as you continue to practice the exercise. For example, you may begin as a newborn, advance to an infant, a toddler, a young child, and so on. Let yourself receive all the love and caring you need to feel safe and protected.

If you scored fairly low on the opening quiz, you'll probably benefit from practicing this exercise daily for 28 consecutive days to lodge the image of a loving inner parent in your deep memory bank. Yes, you can proceed without it, but it will speed your progress toward consistent empathy by giving you a positive counterpoint to any nonempathic examples from your childhood. Children can and do act empathically before they're old enough to have been exposed to canons of right and wrong. *Empathy is based in the body; it's a felt experience.* It's a tug on the heart, a hollow in the stomach, so the best way to get a fresh start on empathy is to *feel* like you have an empathic parent as a model.

You can reinforce the felt nature of empathy by doing the following introspective exercise as well.

DO YOU SPEAK BODY LANGUAGE?

For the next week, take note of how you react whenever you perceive the following in people you encounter:
- A downturned mouth
- A wince
- A sparkle in the eyes
- A lilt in the voice
- A furrowed brow
- A face-splitting grin
- Heavy eyelids
- A shrill tone of voice
- Flaring nostrils

Active awareness should enable you to report with accuracy whenever you feel anything physical. If you've developed some empathy, you'll react to cues from others with some physical sensation of your own, not solely with cognitive recognition of their message. Research on empathy has made much of what's called the ability to read visual cues, but I argue that it's not the cognitive interpretation of the upward or downward turn of an eye or mouth that elicits empathy; rather it's the effect these cues have on us emotionally. When we see a certain facial expression, we remember what happens in the muscles of our own faces as we react to emotional situations, and we recall the emotions associated with these events. The same thing happens when we hear a familiar tone of voice, see someone's skin flush or perspire, or even receive a limp, clammy handshake. Because we feel our own emotions in the body, that's where our empathic responses occur as well.

If you didn't feel anything when you observed those cues, you may need to return to chapter 5 and give your active awareness a jolt. Probably, though, you'll notice a physical response only sometimes—in certain settings or with people who are close or otherwise important to you.

A second possibility is that a cue from someone else sets off a full-blown emotional response in you: When you see anyone crying, you cry, too; when someone else looks gleeful, you're overcome by a fit of giggles. That's not empathy at all. If you can't stay attuned to your own feelings while tuning in to someone else's, you're a victim of one of the most prevalent empathy myths I know.

Clearing Hurdle Two: Rejecting Cultural Myths About Empathy

Being raised in an empathic family is like being born with a silver spoon in your mouth: It's an incalculable advantage in life. Even so, powerful cultural messages can divert us from a heart-directed course.

> *Myth 1: Empathy is too risky—I can't afford
> to immerse myself in someone else's feelings.
> The truth: Empathy is not sympathy.*

Karen and Toni, two members of the same women's group who are both bright and genuinely interested in others, illustrate the difference:

When Karen listens, there are no conversations going on in her head. Her body tells her what she is feeling and also how the speaker feels. When the other person expresses hurt, Karen feels something reminiscent of sadness or pain around her own heart; she feels another's anger as something like an echo of her own anger sensation, in the same area of her stomach. Because she's actively aware, any expression of an emotion from someone else trips a physical sensation almost as quickly as she feels her own emotions in her body. How thoroughly she comprehends the emotion expressed, however, depends on whether the body language used is already familiar to Karen. Having a high EQ doesn't make Karen a mind reader, and it won't make you one, either. But feeling *something* palpable, rather than interacting solely with the cold, clinical mind, is enough to cement the bond between two people; it's enough to make Karen and the rest of us pause for a nanosecond and consider the other person's heartfelt needs before we act.

Just as Karen moves fluidly from attunement to focus on her own feelings, she's able to divert her consciousness from her feelings to those of another without a clunky shift of gears and a concomitant pause. When a group member screws up her face and hunches her shoulders as she begins to speak, Karen feels a degree of anguish because her body feels taut and twisted, too, but she can also determine that she feels strong and unfettered, confident and energetic. That distinction keeps her from confusing the other woman's feelings with her own and being disabled or overwhelmed by emotions that are not hers. Holding on to her own emotional well-being also gives her the wherewithal to do what is truly helpful—not try to make changes in the other person so that she'll feel more comfortable, but remain open to what the speaker really needs.

The person on the receiving end of Karen's empathy feels loved, understood, and supported—and loving and admiring in return.

Toni's intentions are just as good as Karen's, but she hasn't learned active awareness, so she can't listen without getting sidetracked by her own thoughts: "You poor thing." "Isn't that awful?" "I wonder if that could happen to me." "That *has* happened to me." "I want to tell you about what happened to me." "Here's what you should do." Toni too has a physical response to another's emotions, but she can neither keep the event in her body nor stay in contact with her own emotions while chiming in on someone else's. With minimal emotional muscle, she falls prey to fear and shame when a strong feeling echoes inside her, and the internal dialogues commence. Unfortunately they only distance her from the person she's listening to and at the same time make Toni feel uncomfortable. Out of her own feelings of distress come a barrage of suggestions that do little to help the other person. Meanwhile, little or no heart- and gut-level connection takes place, and nothing changes as a result of the exchange.

Those on the receiving end of Toni's sympathy feel disappointed and let down. They wish they had never said anything to her in the first place.

Remember the hilarious *I Love Lucy* episode where Ricky collapses in agony when Lucy begins having labor pains and Lucy has to wheel *him* into the hospital? It's a classic comedy routine and a classic example of how sympathy can dissolve the boundaries between ourselves and others, leaving us unable to distinguish between our own feelings and theirs.

Sympathy of this ilk saps our energy, fuzzes our mind, and rarely helps anyone, but that's hard to see when you're immersed in angst. Take a good look at how well you draw the all-important fine line in this exercise:

CLOSE BUT NOT TOO CLOSE

Repeat the "Do You Speak Body Language?" exercise, but this time take note of (1) what you believe the other person is feeling and, simultaneously, (2) what you are feeling.

Can you honestly report that while you may feel a profound sadness when someone is weeping, you're aware that you are content, even happy? One of the common factors in sympathy, as opposed to empathy, is guilt. It's not right, says the ever-critical IQ, to feel good when someone else feels so bad. *Wrong.* It's not only right but necessary that you continue to feel good (if that's the way you *were* feeling) while also palpably feeling someone else's pain. Here are some other examples of how you might achieve the closeness of empathy without the assimilation of sympathy:

• You can feel a shiver down your spine when someone blanches in fear while remaining cognizant of your own steady pulse and firm, grounded stance.

• You can genuinely laugh along with a boisterous child without feeling disrespectful of the memory of a loved one for whom you are grieving—the joyful swell in your upper chest is perfectly capable of coexisting with the hollow ache you still feel below.

• You can grasp the full import of a loved one's anger toward you without losing the strength of your own convictions buttressed by your sense of positive energy, mental clarity, and regard for others.

If you rarely have experiences like these, but end up feeling the same as the person you're with, you're getting a little too close for comfort—you're confusing sympathy with empathy. To confirm or allay your suspicions, try the following quiz.

❧ QUIZ ☙

To the Rescue?

Think back to the last few times someone caught you off guard by expressing a strong, painful emotion—rage, panic, anxiety, jealousy. If you were truly taken by surprise, your response was probably reflexive and therefore hints at how empathic you really are.

Did you listen with your whole body to find out what the other person really wanted and needed? Were you able to stay silent, outwardly and inwardly, while you waited for a physical response? Or did you leap to the rescue by:

• Offering off-the-cuff advice?
• Trying to convince the person that "it's really not all that bad"?

- Telling the person he or she really shouldn't feel that way?
- Making a joke?
- Changing the subject or suggesting a distraction?

If your instinctive reaction was to do something to stop the person from feeling that way, the only person you were trying to rescue was you. That's not empathy. If you were so overcome by your own answering pain that you didn't know what to do or how to help, you were probably awash in sympathy, not empathy. A few solutions to send you in the direction of empathy follow Myth 4.

Myth 2: Empathy will keep me from doing what's best for me.
The truth: The human heart is infinitely expandable.

People who think that empathy will keep them from doing what's best for themselves are most often driven by fear. They're constantly afraid that feeling someone else's pain will keep them from pursuing their own needs, that if they put energy into being concerned about someone else, they'll lose out on opportunities for themselves. This view of self-interest is suffocatingly narrow and self-centered. Worse, it gives your total intelligence far too little credit. Remember, when you're actively aware, you're attuned to your feelings in the background all the time. You don't have to give up any vigilance to pay attention to others. You have plenty of emotional awareness to go around.

Still, a certain amount of fear can be healthy. You should be comforted to know that empathy will reveal a wolf in sheep's clothing every time. Sometimes you may find yourself feeling that you just don't want to be near someone. At that point if you feel energized, clearheaded, and generally positive, your feelings may be telling you to move out of harm's way. Attuning to other people's feelings may make you privy not just to their pain and suffering but also to their ill will toward you or others. Empathy doesn't make us vulnerable to the harmful influence of others; it protects us from such harm.

Rest assured that a genuine empathic response will never be as painful as the emotion the other person is experiencing. Your body *will* feel an echo of the sorrow, anger, or fear you're witnessing, but it will be diluted. If our bodies were completely taken over by other people's pain, we would never be moved to compassionate acts such as clothing the poor or feeding the hungry. Emotional pain does not offer you anything active to do. That impetus comes from the energy flowing from your own well-being.

Myth 3: Empathy is wimpy.
The truth: Empathy is empowering.

The mistaken assumption is that when my spouse, my mother, my kid, or my coworker asks me to do something—anything—I will do it, even if I don't want to. I'll become one of those people who answers "How high?" after being told to jump. In fact, empathy makes us more assertive and self-aware because it brings us a wealth of information about others and our relationships to them. Knowing what others feel helps us appreciate our individuality. It also motivates and inspires action, making it an empowering resource both personally and socially.

Myth 4: If I let myself be touched by someone's
personal problem, I'll have to fix it.
The truth: People want understanding, not necessarily help.

The assumptions here are that other people's emotions are problems—problems we can fix and problems they want us to fix. In the first place, feelings can be altered only by the person who owns the feeling. In addition, few people really want us to solve their problems and, in fact, most people resent our interfering. What people do need and find helpful is heart- and gut-level understanding. This makes them feel cared for and encourages them to learn from their feelings and solve their own problems. All it takes is listening with your whole body, without composing responses in your head.

Using Your EQ to Put Your IQ in Its Place
What can you do to free yourself from these myths? Quite simply, polish your active awareness. If you passed the final exam in chapter 5, I know you're feeling your body's responses to the emotions of others. Put a little additional practice into active awareness and

you'll turn the volume up on these messages until they're impossible to ignore. Practice Building Emotional Muscle Part III and use the "Mining the Mind" exercises in Chapter 5 to support your effort. At the same time, give yourself an overall checkup: Are you eating, sleeping, and exercising as you should? Are you attending to any problem in your life that's having a negative effect on your energy, mental clarity, and positive regard for others? Consider yourself back in undergraduate school until you notice that (1) you're exhibiting less of the behavior listed in the last quiz, To the Rescue?; (2) in most encounters you can describe a palpable difference between what you feel and what the other person is feeling; and (3) you're comfortable and flexible in your response to the strength of someone else's feelings relative to your own.

Getting Over the Last Hurdle: Preconceived Notions
Chapter 2 discussed the power of entrenched judgments and convictions. Preconceptions can be most stubborn and most dangerous when applied to other people.

Go back to the "Measuring Your Emotional Aptitude" quiz in chapter 2 and fill it in again. This time take all the time you want. You'll probably fill it in differently than you did the first time around, but I'm willing to bet you'll unearth a few stubborn preconceived notions lurking beneath your emotional enlightenment. Undoubtedly they are influencing your encounters with others, preventing empathic behavior. Here's an exercise that can help.

ERASING MIND-SETS THAT BLOCK EMPATHY

If you discover that you find it difficult or impossible to feel empathy for whole groups of people, such as men, women, Republicans, Democrats, rich people, or poor people, use Building Emotional Muscle Part II to explore your feelings about that group. During the middle of the exercise, ask yourself:

1. What do I feel when I picture [insert an individual from the group of people you cannot empathize with]?
2. What is it about that person that provokes this feeling?

As always, understanding the origin of the problem is half the solution. Complete the process by taking a lesson from chapter 4 when interacting with people who fall into this group: When you feel the stab of a disproportionate emotion, breathe fully and deeply, relax, and focus strictly on physical sensation. With repetition you'll create an overlay of positive emotional memory as you have before, gradually opening yourself to empathy for the people you previously judged harshly.

Learning to Balance Your Needs with the Needs of Others

Active awareness is like putting two computers to work on a problem instead of one. Empathy is like having a whole network of PCs at your disposal. As active awareness informs your short- and long-term decisions about what's right for you, empathy informs any decision that affects other people. When you use emotional acuity as well as your other senses to listen, communication becomes productive and efficient. "I get along so much better with my friends these days," says Sheila. "When I say something that bothers someone, I know it right away, even over the phone, and though I don't always understand what's going on, I know enough to ask. Boy, do I save myself a lot of phone calls by finding out then, rather than trying to figure it out later."

Even when you can't react instantaneously, empathy motivates you to rectify a problem because your body urges you to respond to the message that something is wrong. When Stan was put in charge of the construction of a large social service center, several architects on the planning committee had been working on the project for years partially because they intended to bid on it. The first thing Stan did was to solicit additional bids from outside firms, which infuriated the architects on the committee. When they threatened to quit, Stan could have simply stood his ground. After all, his gut feelings told him he'd made the right choice, and his decision held up to logical scrutiny as well. But Stan's being "right" didn't prevent him from deeply experiencing the hurt and disappointment of the people who had given a great deal of time to the project, so he issued a public memo, explaining his reason for going outside the existing group and apologizing for acting unilaterally and appearing ungrateful. Within hours Stan got a call from each architect, thanking him for his apology and assuring him of their full and continued support.

All most people really ask is that we try to recognize what they're feeling and acknowledge that it's just as important to them as our feelings are to us. Empathy makes that possible. When Stan supplied information to someone his business partner was suing, his partner was furious. Stan knew he could have been held in contempt of court for not cooperating, but rather than try to argue the logic of his case, he just listened to how unhappy his partner felt. That's all it took to restore cordial relations between the two men, and the subject was never brought up again.

Not only does empathy free us from labeling one person as right and the other wrong, but it enables us to disagree without being disagreeable. I know one high-EQ woman who can work effectively with anyone because she listens nonjudgmentally, with her body, not just her mind. Awareness of how important others' feelings are and how self-defining hers are as well makes it easy for Marcy to respect vastly differing opinions and values without feeling threatened by them.

Acute sensitivity to the relative weight of people's feelings at any moment in time allows Marcy to juggle conflicting needs so that no one feels oppressed. It also helps her adapt quickly to change. "I was armed with a terrific speech about why my four-teen-year-old couldn't go on a camping trip when he told me, on the verge of tears, that it would be his last chance to see his best friend before the family moved away. It would mean Tom would have no time to study for his math final and he'd miss his grandmother's birthday, but at that moment how he felt seemed so much more important. He went and we all survived."

As you'll discover, empathy is contagious. Sam, a highly effective emotional manager, fell in love with Diana, who resisted Sam's attentions because she didn't think someone of a different race would make an appropriate father for her teenage sons. Though Sam disagreed, he experienced the strength of Diana's conviction and accepted her decision: "Of course you can't marry me believing as you do." Ironically, Sam's ability to let go convinced Diana that he genuinely loved her and would make a devoted husband and father. Empathy has the power to open the hearts of others.

The key is to listen with 100 percent attention. That doesn't mean making soulful eye contact while composing a pithy response in your head. Keep your body receptive to any message that might come in as you train all your senses on the person before you. If that sounds arduous, remember that you don't have to divert mental energy to this task. On the contrary, you need to keep your mind from interfering with emotional signals. If necessary, as always, breathe fully and deeply, relax, and focus to tune your body to the other person's feelings.

Also, remember that other people are solely responsible for their own feelings. You can't expect to divine the feelings of a totally noncommunicative person. Empathy won't make you a soothsayer, a seer, or a sorcerer. It simply ensures that you will perceive any cues sent via speech, gesture, facial expression, and body language. And over time the cues you come to understand add up to significant wisdom. Gestures that no one else would notice may trip a physical signal in you, especially when the sender is someone very close to you. You may even become adept at anticipating how certain people will feel in certain circumstances, but always rely most on *current* feedback. People change over time, and you don't want to pigeonhole them.

How Much Is Too Much to Give?
Some people may prove more difficult to listen to empathically than others, and again you can turn to the Building Emotional Muscle process to stay in your body and out of your head during these

encounters. That's about as far as you can go to solve these transitory problems. Unfortunately, some problems aren't so transitory.

What do you do when someone for whom you feel deep caring and obligation wants more than you can give? Should you visit your aging parents every weekend as they request? Should you spend an hour reading to your daughter before bedtime *every* night? Should you chair the charity fund-raising committee as agreed, now that your job responsibilities have doubled?

Active awareness and empathy can keep you from being strangled by conflicting needs. Chapters 7 to 9 offer more narrowly targeted high-EQ solutions for use in love, at work, and with family. For now, acquaint yourself with empathy's power to resolve even the most vexing conflicts in a way that's emotionally satisfying for all. Becoming a self-sacrificing, long-suffering martyr or a thick-skinned, hard-nosed naysayer will always leave you in a lose-lose conundrum. There *is* a better way.

GIVE AND/OR TAKE

Where in your life do conflicting needs always cause trouble? What periodic events do you consistently anticipate with dread? What encounters always leave you with regrets?

Choose one personal dilemma, perhaps one from the following list, as a research subject and resolve to find a balance between your own needs and the demands of the people around you.

1. The kids are asking for more time with me. How much can I give?
2. My aged parents want me to spend more time with them. How much should I give?
3. My spouse/lover wants more of me sexually. How much should I give?
4. My friend wants me to give him/her more of my time and attention. How much should I give?
5. A coworker has asked me to help out. How much should I give?
6. My community needs help and support. How much should I give?

Experiment with several possibilities to see where on the continuum of possibilities your needs lie. For example, if your parents want you to spend every weekend with them, but doing so leaves you exhausted and your spouse resentful, can you visit them the first and third weekends of every month, devoting the second weekend to downtime and the fourth to whatever your spouse chooses? Can you set aside time to talk to them on the phone daily and spend a very special weekend with them once a month? Can you have them visit you on some weekends to spare you the travel time? Can you split the visits with a sibling?

Obviously you may have to test several possibilities to find the one that leaves you with energy, mental clarity, and benevolence toward others while making the other people involved feel understood and cared for too. Your body will always tell you when you've made a choice that makes someone else happy but leaves you feeling resentful, tired, and oppressed—or one that relieves you of an immediate burden at the expense of your long-term vitality and tranquillity.

You'll recognize that you've found the right balance when what you do for others makes you feel good, too!

From Empathy to Compassion

If there's a consequence connected to empathy, it's that empathy opens our eyes to the suffering of others. Once we become attuned to their feelings, it's pretty difficult to ignore a shivering homeless person, a parent who has lost a child in the crossfire of urban warfare, or a person dying of AIDS.

The link between empathy and caring is obvious. When we experience the suffering of others, we care and want to take action. Daniel Goleman quotes researcher Martin Hoffman as arguing that the roots of morality are to be found in empathy, since in sharing another's distress we feel moved to help. Empathy not only makes us more understanding, loving, and caring parents, friends, lovers, family members, and coworkers, but better citizens of the world. People we don't know—total strangers—begin to matter because when we see or hear about their suffering, we feel we want to respond in some way.

So when I said that adults don't want us to solve their personal problems, I didn't mean it's never appropriate to act in behalf of others. Empathy calls to our attention issues of social need and injustice that require action on our part. Social problems become *our* problems, because with ingrained empathy we really feel we're part of society.

How fully you've become a citizen of the world via EQ is revealed by how far your compassion extends. For those who are interested in exploring the boundaries of their empathy, I offer one last quiz. Your empathy and compassion have the potential for infinite growth over the rest of your life. You might return to this quiz periodically to shed light on how far you've come.

◈ QUIZ ◈

What Do You See in the World That Touches You?

Ask yourself, How do I feel at a gut and heart level, what do I feel like doing, and what do I do . . .

- when I come across a child who looks dirty and poor?
- when I see a parent screaming at the top of his or her voice in public at a child?
- when I see an elderly man who looks homeless?
- when I see an elderly woman who looks homeless?
- when I see a drunken person?
- when I see someone on the street who looks mentally ill?
- when I read or hear about a child who has been sexually abused?
- when I hear or read about people in other parts of the world who are starving?
- when I hear or read about people in other parts of the world who are being tortured and killed?
- when I hear or read about people who have lost their homes or livelihood as a result of natural disasters?

- when I hear or read about a young person with AIDS?
- when I hear or read about a woman who has been raped?
- when I hear or read about a woman who has been beaten and abused?
- when I hear or read about a child who has been physically beaten and abused?
- when I hear or read about older people who have been beaten and abused?

To keep building empathy, don't hide from the world of suffering that surrounds you. Don't try to insulate or isolate yourself from what you see, hear about, and feel in others. Some people try to create protective ghettoes where they won't have to see, hear, or feel the suffering of others. In doing so they not only create a false sense of security but ultimately restrict their capacity for empathy as well.

Final Exam: Do You Use Empathy to Full Advantage?

1. Are you able to put your ego in the background? Can you listen to someone without composing an answer in your head and, at the same time, remain aware of what you're experiencing physically and emotionally?
2. Can you make the distinction between empathy and sympathy?
3. How long can you let someone else speak about himself or herself without needing to say something about yourself?
4. How many sentences can you listen to without having to interject some comment—one, two, three, five, eight? (The longer the better.)
5. Can you let ten seconds elapse before beginning to speak?
6. Can you permit someone to cry for three or four minutes without trying to stop him or her?
7. Is it becoming easier to extend physical comfort to someone who is in pain? Are you comfortable reaching out to

touch someone with your hands? Can you hug someone who feels bad?

✍♥ *If you can answer yes to questions 1 and 2 and to at least three other questions, you can move on to part 2.*

Moving On . . .

Congratulations! You've worked hard at feeling smart, and I'm sure you're eager to leave these hallowed halls and get on with living smart. Part 2 of this book is packed with high-EQ responses to everyday challenges in love, at work, and with family. In chapters 7 to 9 I've distilled the collective wisdom of all the high-EQ souls I have the privilege to know into guidelines for making your life at home, at work, and elsewhere in the world as fulfilling as it can be. Of course, you already have the most reliable mentor there is—the total intelligence of your emotions combined with your intellect.

Use the following chapters as an adjunct or an aid, as a jumping-off point or a handy reference. You'll fill in the framework as you see fit.

Don't be surprised if some of the suggestions in the following pages sound familiar. There's a kernel of emotional truth in many cognitive behavioral techniques and other approaches to personal and interpersonal growth, and that's why they've been around so long. Unfortunately, most are worthless without EQ. It's not difficult to see, for example, that using "I feel" messages is an empty exercise unless you *know* how you feel. So if you've tried any of these ideas in your pre-EQ years and failed to see a lasting benefit, *please try them again now that you have emotional awareness, acceptance, active awareness, and empathy to support your efforts.* I promise that when they're informed by your emotions, freed of fear by acceptance, and catalyzed by active awareness, they can become highly effective tools.

Part 2

LIVING
SMART

7

The High EQ in Love

A god could hardly love and be wise," pronounced Publilius Syrus two thousand years ago. Syrus was wrong. We don't have to choose the wrong lovers, end up in multiple failed marriages, or let the romance seep out of our long-term relationships. We don't have to let conflicting needs and wants come between two people who love each other. We don't have to resign ourselves to boredom or bickering in our love lives.

We have the potential to attain the kind of love we all dream of—deep intimacy and mutual kindness, real committed, soulful caring—simply because of empathy, our innate ability to share emotional experience. But to reach the height of romance we need *all* the skills of a high EQ: astute emotional awareness to avoid mistaking infatuation or lust for lasting love; acceptance to experience emotions that could harm a relationship if left to fester; and vigilant active awareness to apprise us of what's working and what isn't.

Fortunately your EQ need not have peaked before you embark on love. In fact, for many people falling in love serves as the catalyst for reeducating the heart. That's why some of the most deeply passionate lovers I know are in their eighties: They discover that two high EQs add up to a romance that never stops growing, never loses excitement, and always strengthens them both, individually as well as collectively.

Of course, you've got to be able to recognize an opportunity for love when you come across one. EQ can help here, too. As I've said throughout this book, you're not likely to get what you want if you don't know what that is. Emotional awareness can disrupt the hurtful cycle of falling in and out of love by cuing you to exactly how you feel about someone without the obfuscations of what you think—about love, about "your type," about what anyone else expects.

In this chapter I'll give you specific suggestions for staying true to yourself while you're falling in love and for staying truly in love once you've made a commitment to one special person. I'll remind you of when you can use the Building Emotional Muscle process to keep loving smart and which emotional skills you're likely to need most in certain situations. You'll also find some new loving-smart exercises in these pages, many of which are designed for the two of you to use together.

Note, by the way, that "the two of you" does not mean only heterosexual couples. Same-sex couples face most of the same issues that male-female couples encounter and should use the same EQ skills and all the rules of thumb enumerated here. I use the masculine and feminine pronouns only for convenience in this chapter.

That said, every love, like every life, is unique. I can't anticipate the specific challenges you'll face, but I can tell you, from my own romance of forty years and from the experiences of other passionate couples, how to use your EQ to keep love alive and thriving. You have the tools you need to handle many common relationship issues. You have the intelligence to make a lifetime of exciting discoveries about each other and your life together. So the suggestions in this chapter are all built on the unique ways that emotional intelligence equips you to survive where many hopeful lovers have failed. You may have heard them before, but now that you have a high EQ you'll be able to put these lessons to work for you as you never have before:

• *Actively seek change in your relationship.* EQ is the secret of enduring intimate relationships largely because it makes us acutely aware of the changes—large and small—that are constantly occurring in ourselves and others. With the skills you learned in Part I of this book, you'll have the sensitivity that each of us is always seeking in a significant other. You'll automatically sense, through active awareness and empathy, the little shifts in the dynamics of your romance that signal a need for action: Does your lover need something new from you? Do you need to schedule some time to take stock together? Are external influences demanding a change in your respective roles? Are you as happy as you used to be?

Without EQ such questions are often just too scary to face, so many lovers ignore signals of change until it's too late. Instead, when you can ride out your fear of change, you discover that different does not necessarily mean worse. In fact, things often come out better than ever on the far side of change. Relationships are organisms themselves and by nature *must* change. Any relationship not nudged toward the kind of growth you want will drift into change of another kind—maybe one you *don't* want. Your ability to embrace change pays off in courage and optimism.

• *View the challenges you encounter as opportunities rather than problems.* Your courage and optimism, in turn, allow you to view dilemmas not as troublesome problems but as challenging opportunities. How creative can the two of you be? When you don't need to blame each other for your emotions, you're not controlled by negative emotional memories, and you're too alert to keep repeating the same old mistakes—that is, when you have a high EQ, you're liberated from ruts and resignation. You can get down to resourceful problem solving. You can meet differences between you and unavoidable crises as invitations to find each other, challenges to get closer and emerge individually and collectively stronger.

As I said in chapter 6, empathy deepens your appreciation for individual differences but also strengthens the bond of commonality. Why view men and women as speaking different languages or as hailing from different planets instead of as kindred souls with a wealth of emotional experience in common? The language we already share is emotion. Use it to strengthen the link between you and the one you love.

• *Respect all the feelings you have for each other.* We're not always delighted by the discoveries we make about the person we love, but when it comes to emotions it's necessary to accept them all. Being in love doesn't mean never feeling angry, disappointed, hurt, or jealous. How you act on your emotions is up to you; what's important is that you *feel* them. Countless relationships have been ruined by blame; millions of couples have missed out on deep intimacy because of shame. As you know from chapter 4, both are cruel vestiges of unfelt anger, fear, and anxiety. If you've done the work in part 1 of this book, you won't intellectualize these emotions; you'll experience them and get on with your life together.

• *Keep the laughter in your love life.* You learned this in chapter 4, too. To avoid intellectualizing emotions you need acceptance, and a big part of your acceptance comes from laughter. Lovers who can't laugh together about themselves probably aren't very accepting of their relationships and may not be able to tolerate its unique flaws and inevitable stumbles, any more than they can put up with their own. Nor will they be open to a relationship's most pleasant surprises. Your high EQ, in contrast, means you can keep improving your relationship, but you'll never get trapped by intolerant expectations of perfection.

• *Pay attention to how you feel when your lover is not around.* Fortunately, you have a flawless instrument for monitoring exactly how your relationship is faring: Use the three gauges of well-being to figure out how the rest of your life is going. Are you feeling restless or irritable in general? Do you drag through your day at the office or school after a night of conjugal bliss? Do you resent family and friends even though the two of you are spending every available minute alone together? Love never benefits from tunnel vision. If you don't feel energetic, clearheaded, and benevolent *all* the time, it doesn't really matter whether you coo like doves when you're together. If the sex couldn't be better but you're slipping at work, if you feel safe and cozy hearing "Hi, honey" when you come home at night but are having trouble getting up in the morning, something's amiss in Camelot—even though everything feels warm and fuzzy in the castle.

When that happens, all the information about you, your lover, and your relationship that your emotions and your intellect have gathered will steer you to the best solution. If you're new to love and new to EQ, your course will be surer if you remember to stick to these paths:

HeartPaths:
10 Ways to Love Smart

1. *Let the three gauges of well-being inform you about the romantic choices you make.* If you feel energized, mentally clear, and more loving generally, you're in a relationship with a future.

2. *Let your lover know what you feel.* If you're going to communicate anything, express what you feel—it defines who you are. If you pretend to be someone or something you're not, you'll never feel loved.

3. *Listen from emotional experience.* Attune to your lover's feelings as you listen to his or her words.

4. *Show the support and love that your lover needs.* One person may find a suggestion or a helping hand useful or comforting; another person may find the same action intrusive. Not everyone likes to be touched in the same way, enjoys being affectionate in public, or responds the same way to receiving gifts. Let empathy guide you.

5. *When in doubt, ask.* Love doesn't bestow omniscience. If you don't ask how your lover feels about something, you'll never know.

6. *Be prepared to work at the relationship.* Why do so many people believe their work is done once they've found true love? Relationships grow and thrive with attention, or wither and die of neglect.

7. *Learn from your lover.* Active awareness keeps you from relying on past assumptions.

8. *Watch out for emotional memories.* Emotional vestiges of past hurts are most dangerous with those we love today.

9. *Remember that the only problem with making mistakes is not admitting it.* The complexities of relationships guarantee error, but even mistakes are opportunities for growth if met without blame.

10. *Use change as an opportunity to grow your relationship.* Any change is stressful, but it is also an opportunity to renew and revitalize your relationship.

Looking for Love, or How Can You Find the Person You Want If You Don't Know How You Feel?

About half of all American marriages end in divorce, with many of the victims concluding that they simply chose the wrong mate. When you're first falling in love, how can you tell whether this person is "the one"? How do you know whether you're in love with a real person or just in love with love? If you've been burned before, how can you avoid repeating your mistakes?

Listen to your body, not your mind. We choose a mate for reasons that have more to do with what we think than how we feel. We conduct our relationships based on how things should be or have been. And that's exactly where we go wrong. We don't lose at love because we let our emotions run away with us but because we let our *heads* run away with us.

When Molly falls in love, she falls head over heels—and she does it so often that her friends now think of her affairs as predictable seasonable events. Molly says she just "loses her head." In reality her head is in control all the time: Molly is so in love with the idea of love that she never pays attention to how she feels with the latest candidate . . . who inevitably becomes the latest ex.

People *think* they're in love for many reasons—lust, infatuation, desire for security, status, or social acceptance. They *think* they've found true love because the current prospect fulfills some image or expectation. But unless they know how they *feel,* their choice is destined to be wrong.

Whenever your daydreams of a prospective lover take the form of mental debates justifying your choice or otherwise agonizing over it, breathe, relax, and focus to get out of your head and check in with your body. If a feeling that something's wrong persists or grows, your choice is probably wrong.

Jill wants a husband "just like Dad." The trouble is she's already had three who fit that description perfectly, and they haven't made her happy. Perhaps it's time to stop pursuing the kind of man she thinks she wants and instead pay attention to how she feels in the relationship.

If you let mental images versus physical sensation guide you, you'll never know what you really want. Stick to heartpaths 2 and 3, communicating through feeling, to keep tabs on the real you and the real him or her; you may discover you've been deluding yourself about what's important to you and how well this person fulfills your needs. Then follow heartpath 1 and use the gauges of well-being to see how being with this person is impacting the rest of your life. If the prognosis is poor, accept your feelings of loss and avoid blaming the other person for disappointing you.

Heed the messages from your entire body. For most people it's hard to get clear signals from the whole body during new love, because they're drowned out by sexual desire. That's why it's paramount to heed other, more subtle feelings. Muscle tension, migraines, stomach pains, or lethargy could mean what you desire is not what you need. On the other hand, if the glow of love is accompanied by an increase in energy and vitality, this could be the real thing.

If it's more than infatuation or lust, a benefit will be felt in other parts of your life and in other relationships. Follow heartpath 1 and ask yourself these high-EQ questions:

1. Is this relationship energizing the totality of my life? For example, has my work improved? Am I taking better care of myself?
2. Is my head on straighter? Am I more focused, more creative and responsible?
3. Do my "in love" feelings go beyond feeling positive caring for my beloved? Do I feel more generous, more giving, and more empathic with friends, coworkers, or total strangers?

If you have a high EQ, you'll insist that your intended ask the same questions.

If the answers you get from your body aren't what you wanted to hear, try to push beyond the natural fear of loss we all experience. Finding out now that you haven't found true love can spare you the pain of a pile of negative emotional memories—a legacy that can keep you repeating the same mistakes or sour you on love altogether, robbing you of your chance at what Nathaniel Hawthorne called "the one true happiness in life."

To find the person who is really "the one," know the difference between what you can't live without and what you'd like. The following exercise can help.

FINDING OUT WHAT YOU NEED TO FEEL LOVED VERSUS WHAT YOU WANT

1. Focus on your feelings as you've learned to do in the Building Emotional Muscle process. Select five qualities or characteristics in descending order that feel most important to you in a lover. For example: neat, humorous, adventurous, considerate, emotionally open, athletic, attractive, stylish, protective, creative, conversational, smart, affectionate, monetarily successful, well known, well respected, popular, charismatic, maternal/paternal, spiritual, nurturing, empowering.

2. As you consider each characteristic, ask yourself whether it energizes, calms, and stirs you emotionally. Is the experience pleasant, unpleasant, or neutral?

3. A desire will be fleeting or rather superficial, while a need will register at a deeper feeling level.

4. Do the exercise several times to get an even clearer understanding of the differences between your desires and your felt needs in love.

5. Does the person you think you're in love with fulfill these needs?

Take a chance on reaching out. So often we're on guard with someone new that we automatically erect barriers to getting to know each other. Leaving yourself open and vulnerable at this stage of the game can be pretty scary, yet it's the only way to find out if real love is possible between you, and if you're each falling for a real person or a facade. Try being the first to reach out—reveal an intimate secret, show that you can laugh at yourself, risk a show of affection when it seems most frightening. Does the other person's reaction fill you with warmth and vitality? Then you may have found an empathic, kindred soul. If not, you may have found someone with a low EQ and will have to decide whether you want to deal with that (if you do, you'll find some tips in the "When High EQ Meets Low EQ" box on page 172). Either way, you'll learn something you might not have by waiting for him or her to make the first move.

Take the advice of others only when it coincides with what your heart says.

John couldn't help noticing the raised eyebrows, averted glances, and cool tone of voice from friends and family when they were around his fiancée, Anne. Hurt and uneasy but able to extract only vague comments about how "different" Anne is, John has decided to postpone the wedding—so many people who've known him for so long couldn't be that wrong, could they? So busy tuning in to others' feelings that he's tuned himself out, John is about to lose the love of his life.

If John had followed heartpath 1, he would have known that his overall sense of well-being was the authority to rely on, not a dozen well-meaning friends.

Figure out whether you're creating a smoke screen to cover fear of intimacy. Would you answer yes to any of these questions?

- After an especially wonderful experience with my lover, do I find myself wanting less contact with my lover than I usually do?
- Is the only kind of relationship that turns me on connected to an element of danger?
- Do I find myself losing interest as my lover's interest in me grows stronger?
- Do I have to be in control more or all of the time?

If so, my guess is you've been hurt before, possibly badly. So it's no surprise if you're flooded by emotional memories (you're off heartpath 8) whenever a likely prospect surfaces. I'm sure you want to stop the deluge that's keeping you from one of life's most precious experiences, so here's an exercise that may help.

TUNING IN TO FEAR OF INTIMACY

1. Start by doing the beginning and middle parts of Building Emotional Muscle Part 1 as described in chapter 4.

2. Focus on the feelings that come up when you consider making a long-term commitment to your relationship.

3. Ask: "Is this an old feeling? How long have I experienced this feeling? Do I associate this feeling with fear?" If the answer from

your body is in any way yes, then continue by asking, "What am I afraid of?" Possibilities include rejection, abandonment, feelings of inadequacy, loss of control, loss of self.

4. Don't attempt to change or manipulate your feelings—just feel them.

"Right now we can't bear to be apart. Will we still feel this way when we really get to know each other?" Relationships go through stages, and the uninterrupted passion you feel now is part of the first stage. If you use your EQ, though, your love for each other will deepen, erupting into fantastically passionate periods throughout life that are all the better as mutual understanding increases. When your EQ is low, you lose touch with the deeper layers of feeling. You may believe that love is dead unless you feel raging passion all the time. That's what happened to Jeff and Jan, whose heads were turned by flattering and aggressive admirers. Their spouses are gone, and so are their new lovers, whom neither had lasting feelings for anyway.

The key is emotional honesty. Getting to know each other's warts can seem awfully risky, but if you can't reveal your feelings and accept your lover's, you'll be going to a lot of trouble to keep together two people who don't really exist. Keeping up the pretense will become a heavier and heavier burden as time goes on; eventually it will crush you and your love.

To get over the hump of "Will he/she still love me once he/she really knows me?" look to yourself first. Do you have feelings that you can't accept and therefore are afraid to reveal? If so, go back to Building Emotional Muscle Part II and explore them; they may very well be connected to emotional memory that you can offset by using the exercise.

Also, remember that it's never solely up to you. Even soulmates can drift apart if either of you strays from heartpath 6 and is unwilling to work at your love life together. And if your loved one is intimidated by or disapproving of any of your feelings, you may be dealing with a low-EQ person. If that reduces your energy, mental clarity, and benevolence as time goes on, you'll have to do what's necessary to protect your well-being.

Finally, to overcome any fear of closeness, I recommend empathy and humor. Empathy should help you feel your lover's embarrassment or unease and give you some clue as to what support is called for. When you can offer what's needed, you build trust, and the more trust that exists between you, the safer you'll both feel in revealing all your flaws. You've come a long way when you can do some of the gentle self-mocking exercises in chapter 4 together.

Of course, you have to be prepared for the possibility that you'll discover some things you don't like about each other. In that case you can tell your lover the truth about how you feel (heartpath 2) and see what response you get, but I wouldn't count on changing anybody but yourself. Check in with your feelings (heartpath 1) and ask, "Can I live with this permanently?" Loving a person doesn't guarantee that you can live successfully with him or her, and courtship is the time to determine whether any issues are too big to ignore.

If they're little things, empathy alone may make you more understanding and forgiving. The following exercise can also help you prevent the little gripes from piling up.

THE COMPLAINT DEPARTMENT

1. Make a list (I hope it isn't too long) of the things you would like to change about your lover: Don't read the paper when I'm eating with you, clean up when you're with me, don't chew gum, go out with my friends, share more of my interests, etc.
2. Invite your partner to make up a similar list.
3. Look over each other's list. How do you feel about your partner's list? How does your partner feel about your list? How do both of you feel about making some changes?

4. If both of you are emotionally comfortable so far, consider making one or more changes for your partner if your partner is willing to make a change for you. Treat this as a game and you'll avoid turning petty gripes into seething grudges.

Finally, here's an exercise that will help you gauge whether your feelings say you're headed for a permanent commitment. It wouldn't be a bad idea to have your intended do the same exercise and then compare notes. Again, now is the time to find out if either of you has doubts.

IS THIS ENDURING LOVE?: A RESEARCH PROJECT

Spend a few days—perhaps as much as a week—checking out the nongenital parts of your body and asking yourself the following questions. As a result of being in this relationship, when, where, and how do I feel:
• Clearer and sharper mentally?
• More energetic?
• More compassionate?
• More empowered?
• More important?
• More relaxed?
• More comfortable with myself?
• More generous?
• More sensual?
• More giving?
• More appreciative?
• More forgiving?
• More enthusiastic?
• More creative, happier; less critical, judgmental?
If you can't answer when, where, and how to at least 80 percent of these questions, you could be in lust rather than in love.

Making a Life Together, or How Can You Keep the Love You Have If You Don't Know How You Both Feel?

Once you've made a commitment to one special person, will you be able to live happily together through all the years and the changes to come? Will you be able to distinguish the big problems from the magnified little ones? Can you view any problem as an opportunity for growth and put the necessary effort into finding solutions that are right for both of you? Keeping love alive depends on your ability to stay aware of what's important to you, your lover, and your relationship—in the midst of multifarious external demands and the unpredictable vagaries of time. It's a formidable task made possible by the skills of a high EQ. Here are a few ideas for keeping love alive.

Use your imagination. Romance, whether brand-new or ongoing, does not have to make you lose your head. Ardent feeling and clear thinking, you'll find, are perfect bedfellows. When you're trying to keep differences from becoming conflicts that exhaust and defeat you, don't limit yourselves to conventional solutions or ones you've used before. Remember, change is desirable, so don't hesitate to reverse roles—launderer becomes lawn mower, and vice versa; breadwinner becomes homemaker; the usually sexually passive one takes more initiative—and experiments with other ideas. Diligently explore the emotional reactions you both have to anything you try; communicate your feelings via heartpaths 2 and 3.

Remember that we all experience the same emotions. Giving empathy a jump start when the little things are getting to you can be as simple as reminding yourself that you and your beloved are in the same emotional boat. Even though you two may express them differently for cultural reasons, we all have the same feelings. Understanding that irritating or hurtful behavior may be motivated by the same fears and vulnerabilities that you feel can be enough to cut off a nasty retort and inspire a solution.

Don't rest on your EQ laurels just because your relationship is great right now. We all get complacent when things are going well. But if you and your partner let your commitment slide in using EQ in your relationship, you'll become one of the many crisis-oriented couples out there. Be alert not only to change in your partner and your relationship but also to change in your own EQ. If you find yourself falling into blaming ways or evading issues that feel threatening; if you find that familiarity is beginning to breed contempt, don't hesitate to go back to the exercises in chapters 4 to 6.

Understand that any long-term relationship is likely to pass through several stages over time. Earlier in the chapter I stressed that your lives will be unpredictable and that EQ can help you turn capricious change to your relationship's advantage. With or without children, each of you will experience significant changes as you grow older. IQ can help you anticipate the practical realities of these passages; EQ will keep you growing closer and stronger. Whether you're married or committed to each other on your own terms, there is usually a honeymoon phase during which you work out the kinks of living together. Will you take this opportunity to learn each other's language of love and get to know each other, or clam up and start amassing resentments over misunderstandings and little differences? It all depends on EQ. During the early or middle years of your lives together, you'll probably be occupied by careers and financial preparations for the future, and perhaps children, too. Will you let these competitors for your attention kill your romance, or will you delight in the resources you can discover in each other as you grow? What about the later years? The physical limitations of age need not limit the joy you take in each other, but you *will* reap what your EQs have sown: If they're low, you could end up as bored or bitter caricatures of yourselves; high, you can find infinite happiness in your individual and collective wisdom. Here are some of the issues couples commonly wrestle with, in the order you're likely to encounter them.

High-EQ Strategies in Love

"I'm not used to so much intimacy; I'm feeling overwhelmed [maybe even smothered]. What should I do?"

Go back to heartpath 2 and let your lover know how you feel. Your new life together is stressful because it is new, but you could be adding to the stress by withholding your feelings.

People normally have different needs for closeness, but when you're with the one you love and the one who loves you, you can share your normal feelings of jealousy, insecurity, and fear rather than dredging up a way to blame them on your partner and run. Express your feelings and you may find that the person who seems to be causing your fear is the one who can dispel it by showing accepting love for everything you are. Being open here may initiate a frank and intimate talk about what each of you needs to feel loved and supported—heartpaths 4 and 5. If you set the precedent of mutual consideration and honesty now, you'll go a long way toward establishing a bond of trust that will last for life.

The following exercise can be a fun and sexy way to review your evolving needs periodically.

PERSONALIZING THE MEANING OF LOVE AND SUPPORT

1. List five to seven things your lover can do that make you feel loved and supported.
2. List five to seven things that you think make your lover feel loved and supported.
3. Have your lover also do steps 1 and 2.
4. Look over your partner's lists and compare them with yours.
5. Invite your partner to compare his/her lists with yours.

"We both used to laugh when we teased each other. Now we get annoyed and sometimes even fight about the stupidest things. Why do these things bother us now?"

Stick to heartpath 7 and keep learning about each other. Once the honeymoon is over, partners sometimes get overconfident in their knowledge of each other. Maybe you used to think it was funny when your partner teased you about your sense of direction and now every drive ends in a fight. Maybe your lover seemed to like it when you patted her on the behind and made some joking comment about it, but now she considers it a major insult. People end up feeling demeaned and diminished when they can't accept changes in each other's feelings. Perhaps you always felt a little stupid about getting lost, or your partner always felt self-conscious about her ample figure, but each took the teasing from the other as it was intended—affectionately—because you let your active awareness slip a little in the blush of new love. Now that your irritation has grown and is being expressed, however, neither of you can handle these new reactions.

When you feel strongly enough about an issue to express it, deliver a clear "I feel" message to that effect. If your lover seems to be "overreacting" to something you've always done, cut off your own retort by breathing into your empathic feelings so you can understand how important the issue is to him or her.

We're not superhuman, and we have to put effort into getting to know each other—forever. Always use active awareness to judge how *you* feel after you say or do something to your loved one; call empathy into play to listen from emotional experience to his or her reaction—follow heartpath 3. And never hesitate to apologize when you realize you've wronged your lover—heartpath 9.

"It used to be just the two of us, but now the subject of having children is beginning to come up, and we're finding we don't agree. Won't this pull us apart?"

Whether to have children is one of the most emotionally charged issues most couples face—and one of the most complex. There are all sorts of practicalities that need to be considered intellectually, but how each of you feels about the issue is terribly important in sorting out the pros and cons. That's where EQ is irreplaceable. I can't tell you how to make this decision, except to say that if you can't understand and communicate your feelings on the issue, it's bound to pull you apart, no matter what you decide.

"We're spending so much time at work that we hardly ever see each other anymore. How can we be sure we won't lose touch?"

Remain actively aware as you focus on empathy. Have you ever been embarrassed to discover that the dress you bought for your niece is two sizes too small because you chose it for the size she was the last time you saw her? The same thing can happen in love when we're forced to spend time apart, physically or figuratively. Let's say you work at home and are starved for conversation at the end of the day. Your spouse works downtown and is talked out. You get hurt when her response to your "How did everything go today?" is a curt "Fine," and she gets angry when you keep pressing your "sympathetic ear" on her. Now you're both seeking solace elsewhere.

Here's where working at it (heartpath 6) is paramount: It's going to take extra effort to keep track of what's important to each of you when your interests may be diverging and you just don't have much time together. You're going to have to check your values and, if your relationship matters, make listening to both your needs and the needs of your partner a top priority.

Go over heartpaths 4 and 5, asking when in doubt and making sure you're still playing those unique supporting and loving roles for each other now that circumstances are changing. Remember, needs change, and as two people who care deeply for each other, you should be aware of such changes before anyone else. Do you need to do the preceding exercise again?

"Every time we have a slight disagreement, it turns into a fight. What can we do?"

If you've been following all the heartpaths up to now, you should be able to resolve differences without a full-blown fight, unless you're in the grip of an emotional memory.

feeling. Unless you devote quality time to your relationship, you're probably not paying much attention to the other paths toward love. It does take work—heartpath 6—but it's well worth it. Young lovers sometimes laugh at older ones for needing to make appointments with each other, for everything from serious discussions to lovemaking, but when it comes to staving off boredom and other relationship killers, you can't rely on spontaneity. Some couples make a regular date with each other just to review how things are going between them—never mind all their other obligations. The more rapidly your lives together are changing, the more frequently you might consider doing this. Repeat the "Personalizing the Meaning of Love and Support" exercise as part of your agenda and try the problem-solving exercises again, if necessary.

This, of course, is not to suggest there's no place for spontaneity in your love life. In fact, this is where your imagination should shine. A new activity, a great vacation, some change in your daily routine, a role reversal—all can keep things intriguing. But sometimes all it takes to spark interest and renew passion between you is a tiny surprise. Can you bring home a takeout dinner from a cuisine neither of you has ever tried? How about putting on a favorite CD and whisking your spouse into a dance? What about offering to read a story to your worn-out, bleary-eyed partner some evening? What you already know about your loved one will give you ideas, especially if you polish up your empathy by refreshing your active awareness (see chapter 5).

Don't forget that your active awareness will also point to problems outside your love life that may be causing boredom within it. Maybe you're not bored with your romance but your job or your home routine; maybe it's your body that's languishing and you need a new exercise routine. Explore all possibilities; use the "Give and/or Take" exercise in chapter 6 to see how you can best satisfy the needs of both you and your partner.

"Can we lovingly respond to the physical and health changes that take place in advanced age?"

Follow heartpaths 2 and 3, communicating with and listening to emotion. People who keep information flowing between them can handle virtually any change that life throws them. If arthritis makes some sexual activities impossible, talk to each other about trying others. If a hip replacement means tennis is out, your empathy can help you understand that the debility is your partner's, not yours, and stave off resentment. When serious health problems arise, you can be a source of endless strength to each other if you keep talking, listening, and laughing together.

HIGH EQ IN HABITS OF LOVE

What is the likelihood of staying in love for forty, fifty, or sixty years? Look over list A and list B and check off the items with which you identify most.

List A

_____ I know how to take care of myself emotionally.

_____ The happier, more fulfilled, excited, and satisfied you are, the more loving you will be toward me.

_____ I care for you because it's fun and feels good.

_____ The better you feel about yourself, the better you'll feel about me.

_____ Being in a relationship with you makes me feel better about myself.

_____ I could live without you, but life is so much sweeter living with you.

_____ I know that you could live without me, but you would rather live with me.

_____ I'm not afraid to tell you that "I love you."

_____ It gives me pleasure to show you my love.

_____ I don't expect you will always agree with me or take my side.

_____ I know that what I get out of our relationship depends on what I put into it each day.

_____ Important decisions are made by consensus; if either one of us is really unhappy it won't work in the long run.

_____ I know you care about how I feel.
_____ You know I care about how you feel.
_____ I'm not afraid of change; I look forward to it.

List B

_____ I expect you to take care of me emotionally.
_____ I take care of you because I should.
_____ If you feel too good about yourself, you'll leave me or not need me.
_____ Being in a relationship with you makes me question myself.
_____ I couldn't live without you.
_____ I want you to believe that you couldn't live without me.
_____ If I tell you I love you, I'll be in your control.
_____ If you love me, you will agree with me and always take my side.
_____ If I confide in you, you'll use what you know against me.
_____ I'm not interested in your feelings.
_____ When love is real, you don't have to keep investing in it.

If you checked off more statements on list B than A, you've probably disconnected from active awareness. Go back to the suggestions following the "Recognizing Disconnection" quiz in chapter 5 to devise a remedial program.

Now do the same exercise, checking off the statements you assume your partner would pick. Compare notes. You may learn a lot about hidden fears you both hold and mistaken assumptions about each other. Identifying these beliefs now can spare you trouble in the future.

WHEN HIGH EQ MEETS LOW EQ
DEALING WITH A LOW-EQ LOVER

We don't all grow emotional muscle at the same rate. If you're ahead of the one you love, here are some high-EQ ways to respond to low-EQ behavior.

Getting a message across to a lover who has a hard time hearing. Melba says, "I want to talk," and Pete turns on the TV. For years Agnes has been telling Harvey to brush his teeth before making love to her, but he keeps forgetting. Every night Carl comes home from work and gets upset with Ruth because she's torn ads out of the paper before he's had a chance to read it.

High-EQ responses to poor listeners:

1. Take time to consider the feelings as well as the words that you want your partner to hear. If you're not clear about what you need and why you need it, your message may be garbled. Use the Building Emotional Muscle process if you're unsure of exactly what you want to say.

2. Select a time when you and your partner are not rushed or hassled. Take a walk together or make a date for brunch or dinner, but watch the alcohol if you want him or her to remember the discussion.

3. Send "I feel" messages—about *your* needs—if you want your partner to hear that something is wrong with him or her. For example, "I feel like making love more often, but I have this thing about the odor of onions and garlic, so would you be willing to brush your teeth before coming to bed?"

4. If your partner reacts defensively to the feeling you've expressed, repeat his or her concerns: "You're afraid that if I take this job you and the kids will be neglected."

5. Repeat your "I feel" message, then listen again and keep up the process until you're satisfied you've been heard.

Saying no when your partner takes it personally. If your lover is hurt and feels rejected when you say, "No, I don't want to go to the game with you," "No, I won't go with you to your mother's every weekend," "I don't want to be disturbed," or "I don't intend to stay home with you this evening," try phrasing such statements with clear "I feel" messages and empathy:

- "No, I don't want to go to the football game with you. I don't enjoy doing that—but by all means go and have a good time."
- "No, I won't go with you to your mother's every weekend. I understand why you want to go that often, but I don't feel as motivated as you do. I would rather go every two or three weeks."
- "When you see my workroom door closed, that means I don't want to be disturbed. The interruptions frustrate me by slowing me down and preventing me from getting my work done."
- "I'm going to have dinner with a friend even though I know that you would like me to be home in the evenings. I love you and enjoy your company, but it's very important to me to pursue my own interests."

Waking up a daydreamer. Many people raised with a low EQ space out when confronted by intimacy or any strong feeling. Their lovers end up feeling discounted and hurt. There's only one way to shake him (sorry, but most daydreamers of this ilk are men) out of his reverie: Really show him your pain—not your anger, blame, or contempt, but your hurt. If you've built emotional muscle, you should be able to show your daydreaming lover how deeply his retreat hurts you. If he loves you, he may be motivated to change.

A Paradigm for Loving Smart

Sally and Hank recently celebrated their fortieth wedding anniversary. On their first date Sally showed up in jeans, Hank in his best suit. Laughing while they ran down a list of places where both would be dressed right, they ended up buying a picnic dinner and listening to the free concert in the park, where Hank took off his jacket and tie. More and more over the next year they couldn't wait for weekends, when they could share their work successes—which were mysteriously multiplying—and their war stories. Hank learned that Sally didn't want his advice about handling a problem at work unless she asked for it; Sally learned that the reason people seemed to go out of their way to do things for Hank was the way he spoke and listened to everyone with the same courteous consideration. She felt like she was on top of the world when she used the same empathic approach with a difficult customer and made her biggest sale ever. The first thing she did when she got home was rush to the phone to call Hank.

Soon they were making wedding plans and spending their weekends talking about their future together. Hank, an only child, wanted a large family; Sally said she wouldn't be ready for years. Both agreed she should continue working and finishing her education at night before they talked about it again. Sally wanted to live in the suburbs, Hank in the city. They agreed on the city until their kids were born. Hank wanted to live in his aging parents' neighborhood so he could be on hand to help when needed; Sally preferred to put some distance between them. They compromised on the distance and agreed on Thursday night dinners as a family as long as Friday nights were exclusively their own.

When Sally graduated, Hank brought up children again, but Sally was desperate to have a few years at work in her new field before tying herself to the home. Three successful years later Sally hesitantly agreed to start a family, but two years passed without a pregnancy. Sally secretly felt guilty for having waited, and Hank tried to hide how distraught he was becoming over the possibility of never becoming a father. Their evenings began to alternate between cold silence and door-slamming fights, until one day Hank punctuated an argument with "If *you* hadn't been so selfish for so long, this wouldn't be happening." Sally whirled to shout back but instead burst into tears and then whispered, "I know." Hank was immersed in sorrow when he felt Sally's guilt and shame, and they stayed up all night talking about what they'd both been feeling for ages. Finally they agreed to stop trying to conceive and adopt a child. Two months before the adoption was to occur Sally conceived their first child, a son. She quit her job, and two years later their second son was born; three years later they had a daughter.

Sally's family kept her busy, but more and more she felt something was missing in her life, that her work at home wasn't using all she had to offer. So when her older son was twelve she told Hank she wanted to go back to school to prepare for a new career in social work. "I can't go back to school without your help and support," she said. "It will mean more work and responsibility for you. Will you do it?"

Hank felt scared—he would miss Sally's time and attention—but could feel how important it was to Sally to explore new horizons, so he said yes. Their new schedule meant they were busier than ever, but the excitement both found in their new ventures brought new happiness as well. As Sally dove into her schoolwork with relish, Hank found that mastering the art of home-made pasta and reading his favorite stories to the children refreshed and energized him after his own day at work. Late-night conversations in which Sally and Hank shared all their new experiences were the best they'd had in a long time.

As their children grew up, the couple had more time for making new friends, investing in community projects, and spending quiet, relaxed time alone. Romance blossomed, and both felt they had never been more contented. A few years later, however, they faced the greatest challenge of their lives when Sally was diagnosed with breast cancer.

Sally and Hank spent a few days in stunned silence, swallowed up by fear. Then one morning Hank finally broke the ice. "I feel so helpless," he confided. "What can I do?" "I don't know," Sally answered, "I've never been thorough anything like this before. Can I tell you one day at a time what I need?"

And that is how they lived for the next year—one day at a time, while Sally underwent the rigorous treatment meant to save her life. Sally used her ability to focus on her feelings to give her doctors precise feedback about how her treatments were affecting her. She did the same with Hank when she told him, "I can't bear that worried look you've been carrying around with you. It's not your fault, but it makes me feel like I'm already dead. I need your strength, your old laughter and sense of humor. It may sound crazy, but I want you to play with me."

Hank was delighted and relieved to have something constructive to do for Sally. The first thing they did was spend an afternoon at the zoo, where they ate popcorn and talked to the animals.

After eight years Sally was pronounced cancer free and remains so to this day. On their fortieth anniversary their children asked them the secret of choosing the right mate. "Find someone you can talk to," said Sally. "Find someone who will listen," said Hank.

8

The High EQ at Work

We need EQ most where we're least likely to find it: at work.

The workplace remains the last bastion of IQ worship because many people still believe that getting personal interferes with productivity. Treating fellow workers with empathy and understanding, they fear, will only put individuals' welfare where the company's welfare belongs—at the top of everyone's priorities.

If you've done the work in part 1 of this book, you already have an inkling that being "all business"—meaning all intellect—will get you nowhere fast. In reality, interpersonal skills are critical in the workplace.

At work you don't have the ties of love to motivate you to get along with others as you do at home. You don't often have the benefit of a shared history to help you understand what moves those around you. That makes it all the more important that you have a way to tune in to what those you work with need right here, right now. You do have that facility—it's active awareness and the empathy that flows from it.

In this chapter I'll tell you how to use those elements of your EQ to achieve success and solve problems on the job. Office politics, morale problems, and lack of cooperation don't have to ruin your work life if you can read and respond to people's feelings.

Of course, awareness of your *own* feelings is just as essential on the job. Knowing how you feel will help you develop integrity and find personal fulfillment at work. But it will also make you sharper than ever. I'll show you how to unthrone IQ by proving to yourself and those with whom you work that intuition is a valuable factor in decision making and should always be trusted. And I'll demonstrate how the lightning-fast feedback of your emotions gives you the foresight and flexibility to stay on top of change.

Whether you're working with products or people, EQ offers you the chance to make the most of your work. Let's start by getting you the right job.

Is Your Work "Love Made Visible"?

No matter what your occupation, work is rarely "just a job." As poet Kahlil Gibran said, "Work is love made visible." It's a way to transform your passions and principles into tangible creations, a way to join with your fellow human beings in the noble endeavor of leaving behind a better world than you found.

That's why your work must have some type of personal meaning for you. The daily business of doing business often matters a lot more than the financial security, leisure benefits, and social status that flow from a "good job."

Fortunately, EQ gives you a way to know how healthy your job is for you and which of your fundamental needs it satisfies or fails to satisfy. Knowing which job events put a spring in your step and which send you home dragging like a sick puppy can motivate you to leave a toxic work environment. It can help you distinguish surmountable job frustrations from irreconcilable differences, the need for a vacation from the need for a new career. If you do look for a new position, attunement to internal and external nuances delivers intuitive messages that can lead you to the right job: The perqs and the job description may seem perfect, but if you feel uneasy, uptight, or otherwise uncomfortable in your prospective surroundings, you'll know you should keep looking.

Even when economic need and other practical realities force you into a job situation that falls short of your ideal, you can use your emotions to remain in control and attain contentment in the workplace. And taking charge of the factors you *can* control leaves you emotionally and mentally free to grab the new vocational opportunities that life's passages inevitably present. So use the following high-EQ exercises to take the pulse of your job satisfaction, now and for the rest of your life.

✍ QUIZ ✍

Job Satisfaction: Is Your Work "Love Made Visible"?

Stay in your body as you quickly and spontaneously check off the statements that represent your feelings about your job:

____ I look forward to going to work.
____ I feel challenged at work.
____ I feel appreciated at work.
____ I like being with my coworkers.
____ I leave work feeling tired but good.
____ I feel respected at work.
____ I feel a sense of camaraderie at work.
____ I feel healthy at work.
____ Work feeds my self-esteem.
____ Work is fun.
____ Work brings our the best in me.

If you found yourself agreeing with more than half of the statements, you can probably skip this section and move on to page 193 and the specific advice for problem solving in the workplace. But if your body says you're not as happy at work as you thought, it's time to find out what's wrong. Start with the following exercise.

EXPLORING DISINTEREST IN YOUR JOB—PART I

1. Breathe and relax as in the beginning of the Building Emotional Muscle exercise (page 58).
2. In the middle of the exercise, focus on your feeling of discontent—perhaps numbness, nonfeeling, or depression.
3. Allow the feeling to intensify as usual.
4. Question your feeling: Is this an old feeling? If not, when did I first experience this feeling? Is this feeling related to work alone or to other parts of my life as well?

It's not unusual for people to discover through this exercise that their dissatisfaction really has nothing to do with work. When something feels off in your life, it will affect your energy, mental clarity, and regard for others in all settings. So just as a bad work situation can damage your home life, for example, problems at home can seep into the workplace. If family demands or crises make it impossible to perform well at this job, you may have to seek employment that allows you more leeway. It's also possible, though, that the "High-EQ Workplace Strategies" beginning on page 189 could help you cope at work even if home problems don't abate.

Or you may find out work *is* your whole problem. In that case, if you're well practiced with the exercise, you might know right away what's causing your discontent, and you can use the exercise to engage in creative problem solving: Picture the problem solved and focus on how you'd feel about the job then. If your discontent disappears, you know you need to work on solving that particular problem; see if any of the strategies beginning on page 189 help. If it remains, explore further, such as with Part 2 of the exercise.

EXPLORING DISINTEREST IN YOUR JOB—PART 2

The following is a list of common occupational complaints. Read through them and note any that evoke the same strong feeling of discontent you explored in Part I.

- No one is interested in my ideas.
- They don't appreciate me at the office.
- My boss is rigid and inflexible.
- The job doesn't challenge me.
- I don't understand what my boss wants from me.
- Nobody listens to me.
- My supervisors make unreasonable demands.
- My coworkers are unfriendly.
- The goals that the higher-ups set are unreasonable.
- They treat me like a slave.
- I'm always the last to hear when my staff has a problem.
- Nobody wants to work hard these days.
- Nobody will do anything without asking, "What's in it for me?"
- They can't see the forest for the trees.
- I'm never given the tools I need.
- My boss plays favorites.
- There is no leadership here.
- There is no sense of mission.
- There is no consistency.
- Everyone around here is so busy covering his ass that no one ever gets anything done.
- My boss doesn't understand that my family needs me, too.

Minor complaints may elicit a passing twinge of irritation, but a real problem area will evoke a deeper, prolonged feeling. It may make you feel uncomfortably restless—your body is telling you that you want to shake off something that has bothered you repeatedly. If none of the complaints gives you a clue, explore other possibilities by making sure you stay actively aware at work, using the exercises under "Mining the Mind" in chapter 5 if helpful. Can you identify your low-energy points in the day? The times when you lose your concentration? What happens right before you start snapping at people? With concentrated effort you should have a good idea of what feels wrong at work within a couple of weeks.

If it's a practical matter, concerning hours, logistics, or remuneration, you'll find suggestions on how to negotiate for what you want from the job later in this chapter. If, on the other hand, you discovered that your organization's values don't gibe with yours, its goals don't inspire you, the field bores you, or you're stagnating in the job, it's time to explore other jobs or careers.

FOLLOWING YOUR DREAM—PART I: IDENTIFYING YOUR PASSIONS

If you could choose whatever work you wanted, what would it be? Ask yourself, "What would I rather be doing?" and let your imagination experiment with a variety of scenarios. Let images and ideas flow naturally; don't censor anything at this point, no matter how farfetched it may seem. To get your imagination going, ask the following questions:

* What is my dream job?
* What did I envision myself doing when I grew up—at the age of 5, 10, 16, 21?
* What did I like most about previous jobs?
* What do I do during my time off?
* What kind of help do I instinctively offer to people?
* What's the hardest work I've ever done that made me feel energized, not exhausted?
* Where do I prefer to spend my days—indoors or outdoors, in an office or a workshop, alone or with people?
* What skill have I always wanted to learn?

Use your body and mind to recognize feelings of joy, contentment, usefulness, and compassion as you generate random ideas. Follow your most intense *feelings*, as you do in Building Emotional Muscle. Ignore, for now, any fantasy with no feeling attached to it. The best employment consultant I know concentrates on what the client's passions in life are, and you can do the same for yourself. Whatever stirs you emotionally will suggest a direction for the future. Later you can review your ideas and hunches more methodically; you can also use the next exercise to narrow down your list.

FOLLOWING YOUR DREAM—PART 2:
WHAT ABOUT THIS JOB IS MOST FULFILLING?

1. Use the Building Emotional Muscle process to deeply relax your body and focus on your physical experience. Experience yourself at work in your imagination. What are you doing? How do you feel?

2. Try out different scenarios and see how they feel to you. What part of your job feels best? Don't settle for the first picture that comes to mind; wait until something comes that really feels good. Remember to look for the answers within your body.

3. If, after you repeat this exercise several times, the same idea or image comes up, take it seriously.

Uncovering a dream that's been bubbling under the surface of your vocational aspirations can be very exciting, especially if fulfilling it seems feasible. Jane, for example, discovered that her favorite part of her accounts receivable job was figuring out which clerks were best suited for which tasks. A couple of inquiries uncovered an opening in personnel, and that's where she is today. If your dreams seem harder to realize, remember that EQ will tell you when you've found fulfillment where you may not have expected it. Awareness of your feelings gives you the flexibility to take other avenues to vocational fulfillment.

1. Follow your dream outside your paying job. If you don't want to or can't abandon this job, consider volunteer work or recreational outlets for your dream. A would-be executive may find fulfillment as executive director of a civic organization; a waitress may be able to do her job happily because of the joy she reaps from community theater work; an accountant may be able to fulfill his dream of using his hands by helping with crafts projects at a local school or Y. Many people find that volunteer work is also a great place to make mistakes: Skills they learn in these endeavors gives them the experience and training to achieve what they wanted all along in their jobs.

2. Watch for opportunities to fulfill your dream at one of life's passages. Psychologists and sociologists often divide the human life span into stages to acknowledge how our needs change over the years. These passages afford new opportunities to fulfill your dream. A change in your own life can mean not only new career possibilities but also perhaps a new perspective on any risk that has seemed prohibitive in the past. If getting married means moving to a new city, maybe this is your chance to try a new field. If the kids have finally graduated from college, it may be your turn to go to school. If having children means doing without your salary anyway, why not take a risk on the entrepreneurial enterprise that's always intrigued you?

3. Remember that even our fondest dreams change. While you're contemplating such possibilities, don't forget to consider this one: Your dream may not have grown along with you. To make sure you stay abreast of any changes in it, repeat the preceding exercises whenever a major change in your life occurs. Maybe you'll find you still aspire to being a fearless leader but no longer envision yourself doing it at this company or even in this field. Would you feel successful as a bigger fish in a small pond or a smaller fish in a bigger pond?

Anticipating life stages and passages can be helpful, but only emotional awareness will keep you abreast of the changes *you* undergo. As you age, it's crucial to know how integral work is to your sense of self-worth so you can avoid the feeling of uselessness that often results from our society's obstinate embrace of a retirement age that's premature in light of today's life expectancy. Will you feel vital and productive only if you continue to earn an income? If so, entrepreneurial enterprise may be the path for you. If not, how about volunteer work? Use the preceding exercises to help you decide.

From Self-Fulfillment to Group Fulfillment

Lifetime job fulfillment depends on maintaining an undercurrent of self-awareness, but without the interpersonal skills that encourage cooperation, harmony, and mutual respect, no one achieves the objectives that propel us up the career ladder. The most influential people in any organization are always those who understand not only how they feel but also what motivates their employers, employees, and coworkers. Here are a few precepts to help you apply your emotional intelligence to fostering cooperation and communication in the workplace.

Remember that we all share the same emotions. Many organizations are severely crippled by people devoting more time to protecting themselves from real and imagined threats than to working. When fear rules, productive hours are lost in attempts to keep the upper hand, dodge the boss's wrath, or jockey for position. The undeniable fact that some people have more power than others in any organization does not have to overwhelm you with fear in the workplace as long as you remember that everyone feels the same emotions—and everyone attempts to avoid feeling in the same ways. Does your manager act like a tough guy because he's afraid being compassionate means being weak? Are your employees sullen because they feel just as demeaned as you would if no one showed appreciation for their work? Does the woman in the next office snap at you because she's just as worried about rumored layoffs as you are? When you remember that we are all peers on an emotional level, it becomes so much easier to approach the boss, to ask an employee to give a little more, or to understand that a coworker's irritability is nothing personal. Emotions are great levelers among people; use them to tie you together rather than rend you apart.

Remember that we all need to feel valued and needed. How long do you think you'd last in a job that seemed to have no intrinsic worth, where you didn't feel valued by those around you? I've known people who've endured imbecile employers because the organization furthered a worthy cause and people who've stayed in secretarial jobs well past traditional retirement age because their boss made them feel so deeply needed and appreciated. Few of us can hope to save the world through our jobs, but when we interact with people who make us feel valued and cared for, we feel good about ourselves and are inspired to work harder, longer, and more creatively. And when we make others feel valued and cared for, we get the kind of support we need to do our jobs well. Whether you're dealing with an employer, an employee, or a coworker, taking pains to show appreciation and to ferret out someone's hidden talents will be repaid a thousandfold.

Seek teamwork and cooperation. Industrial psychologists have known for years that people working together are more efficient and productive than the same number of individuals working separately. Competition that pits several teams against each other invariably results in all teams doing better than when single people vie for a prize against one another. Empathy encourages us all to work cooperatively.

If you're the boss, make it worthwhile for your staff to rely on and assist each other: Offer bonuses or other incentives for group rather than individual achievements. Hold TGIF lunches and periodic morning bagel fests on you—sometimes *without* you—so your group can feel free to establish the common ground of griping about the boss. Set up a mentor program matching new employees with those with the greatest seniority. Use your incisive emotional powers to offset one person's weaknesses with another's strengths, and soon they'll all be pulling one another up to new heights.

Employees can prevent a toxic "every man for himself" atmosphere from forming by extending empathic offers of help, staying alert for opportunities to yield when an issue is more important to someone else than to themselves, and simply showing interest in one another's work and lives. Avoid gossip and cliques; both create tension and mistrust, lower morale, and reduce productivity.

Be proactive, not reactive. Constantly missing the boat is tremendously demoralizing in an arena where reflexes are expected to be sharp and foresight is highly valued. If the only action you ever take at work is a reaction, you'll miss opportunities, waste time, and generally fail to advance. Fortunately, EQ not only makes your reactions sure and quick but also helps you foresee internal and external problems, nip conflict in the bud, and avoid getting stuck on plateaus. When you're not devoting all your energies to cleaning up existing messes, you free yourself to make truly innovative improvements. It's flawless awareness that turns managers into brilliant strategists and leaders into visionaries.

Trust your intuitive feelings. Our feelings come to us before our thoughts, yet we've learned to distrust our intuition in the workplace unless we can gather intellectual support for it. As many smart investors, marketers, and designers will attest, stock market killings, media blitzes, and new product development often depend on hunches. There isn't always time for methodical gathering of data. Nor is there always a need. Your hunches, after all, are the product of instantaneously gathered and sorted emotional information that tells you what matters most to you in any situation, what might be wrong based on your previous experiences, and when something is not what it seems to be. Heeding them is not taking a crazy risk as the IQ minions would have you believe. It's often the smartest, most responsible move you can make. You may get a lot of opposition, but stand firm and follow your hunches. Without them you lose the ability to switch gears, grab opportunities, and respond to emergencies.

Never let your emotions fester. The influence of low-EQ intellectuals, the pressure to perform or decide before you feel ready, and the natural fears that arise where your family's security is at stake can make it difficult to stay out of your head when intense emotions come up at work. *Do whatever is necessary to stay in your body and ride out those emotions.* If left to fester intellectually, they'll dull your intellect and your reflexes and start a new pile of negative emotional memories. Take a break and head for the restroom, stroll through the building, or close your office door for a moment whenever you feel you might be overwhelmed; use the Building Emotional Muscle process to focus, even for just a minute. If that's out of the question, be sure to explore the feeling at a more relaxed pace when you get home.

HeartPaths: 10 Ways to Work Smart

With these precepts held close to your heart, you can be a paradigm of self-awareness and empathy on the job, but you're still bound to run into many people who have the interpersonal skills of Attila the Hun. Even a dream job can turn into a daily nightmare. What can you do? Look to yourself. You can't expect to change anyone else, but when you attend to your own EQ, you stay in control of your job satisfaction. Here are ten ways to stay happy and productive on the job.

1. *Use your body to sharpen your mind.* Along with adopting good health habits generally, spending about twenty minutes exercising once or twice a day adds energy, sensitivity, patience, flexibility, and creativity to your portfolio.

2. *Invite feelings as well as output.* Make it safe for people to tell you how they feel and they'll work harder and better. People tell the truth to those who withhold judgments, keep confidences, and maintain their composure; make sure that describes your work persona.

3. *Establish emotional boundaries.* Intimacy with a boss, employee, or coworker can flood the workplace with emotional memories that cause thoughtful, reasonable professionals to lose their objectivity and provoke resentment in onlooking coworkers.

4. *Make no decision based on data alone.* Before you turn in that figure-filled report or cite an authority to back up your recommendations, use your intuition: Stop and ask yourself how you feel about the position you're taking—it's a habit that will imbue your opinions with conviction and integrity.

5. *Be flexible.* Be ready to modify long-term goals based on active awareness of how short-term objectives are going. Stubbornly charging toward ends that no longer serve the organization will get you left behind with yesterday's news.

6. *Be generous.* When a point of conflict means more to the other person than you (information you receive through awareness and empathy), yield graciously; you'll earn your coworkers' gratitude and support.

7. *Begin any negative comment with a positive one.* You're much more likely to get an empathic ear if you preface criticism with appreciation, and complaints with your intention to cooperate.

8. *Speak out when you feel something is important.* If a problem or a conflict is bothering you at a gut level, waiting too long to speak up will invite emotional flooding. You may not elicit a change in the troublesome person or situation, but when you take action you change how you feel about the problem, which has a powerful impact on your well-being.

9. *Listen with empathy; using your emotions will never distract you from the task at hand.* Empathy gives you instant understanding of what someone is saying, so don't try to save time by planning what you're going to say while another person is speaking—that's not heartfelt listening, and others know it.

10. *Take the risk of appearing imperfect.* High performers ask for help when they need it and admit to being wrong when they make a mistake. Then they move on, effective and efficient.

High-EQ Workplace Strategies

Because our shared emotions are such a great leveler, these heartpaths apply to everyone in the workforce, from business owner to temporary help. Still, reality dictates that the managers in the workforce face somewhat different dilemmas from those they manage, so I've divided the following strategies by workplace roles. I strongly suggest that everyone read them all.

Being a Great Boss Through EQ
Like it or not (and many in supervisory positions do not), if your job involves managing other people, they'll view you as their fearless leader. That means that even if they've been raising their

EQs, too, they'll look to you to initiate action, elicit communication, and set the style and pace of daily operations. Here's how you can meet their expectations and get them to meet yours:

• *Anticipate people problems.* Use your empathy to know your employees and how they interrelate. With it you understand what motivates individuals, what relationships have formed, and even the separate "personality" of the organization or department. With active awareness of change you spot problems a mile off. Will your department's rising star begin to fall now that his mentor has retired? Will a reorganization remove critical support systems? Will turning a project over to a consultant be a relief or an affront to your staff? The more you know about how they feel, the less often your own actions will inadvertently create havoc. Remember heartpath 5.

• *Be the first to speak.* Even if you've created a safe and open atmosphere for communication via heartpath 2, some people are intimidated by the boss and won't bring up a problem before it's exacted a hefty toll. Herald any change with a frank talk about potential problems and invite comment. If you sense discontent, broach the subject in a way that assuages that employee's insecurities; then respect the person's privacy if he or she declines to talk.

• *Make it known that you're always ready for employees to improve themselves.* We energize our world of work by looking for strengths in others. Working people have hidden talents that can be used for the benefit of all: Can your receptionist turn a boring memo into an eye-catching flyer with her artistic talent? Can your mailroom supervisor design a new storage room configuration? Nothing builds morale better than noting the value in others. Let your employees know that you're open to their reaching as far as they can, and they'll probably aim higher.

• *Offer only as much as you intend to give.* Don't invite comment if you don't intend to follow heartpath 9 and listen wholeheartedly. Never hold out the promise of rewards if you can't deliver. Don't hold brainstorming sessions and tell your staff how brilliant their ideas are if you never intend to put any of them to use. Adults recognize lip service when they hear it and don't work very hard for those they don't trust.

• *Model flexibility and adaptability.* If you want your employees to be creative self-starters who work up to their potential, show them that responding to contingencies effectively is more important than sticking to rigid plans and rules. Can you toss out a game plan that isn't working without worrying about how it makes you look? Can you react quickly to reports of problems by your employees? Can you regroup and restrategize without acting put out?

• *Cultivate employees; don't coddle them.* Despite what some retrograde managers believe, you can listen to your employees and show concern for their feelings without babying them. Remember, empathy is different from sympathy (see chapter 6), and you must keep attuned to your own feelings while attempting to understand theirs. With a high EQ you'll be able to cut off a heart-to-heart talk before it becomes unproductive and interferes with your own goals, without offending your employee. You'll be able to praise people for a job well done without fearing that it will result in a relaxed work effort or a demand for a raise. You'll be able to balance your employees' need to be valued with your need to achieve goals. Your emotional acceptance (see chapter 4) will keep you from being manipulated by someone else's distress.

"I manage a small agency where everyone is needed every day. How can I respond fairly to employees' needs for time off or flex time?"

Good managers are flexible and welcome change, not only the changes they impose but the changes employees need to make. So if you value the employee making the request, you'll try to view it as an opportunity to be creative and respond by first acknowledging the person's value to the organization. Then use emotional awareness and empathy to gather all the data you can before offering a solution: Does the person really want a change or just a chance to tell you about a problem? Does the person want you to solve the problem, or would he or she feel better if challenged to work out a solution by negotiating for help or tradeoffs with coworkers? Empty your head while you listen to find out. If it's up to you to offer a solution, don't speak until an idea feels good. At work that will generally be the one that makes you look happily ahead to the next challenge at hand.

"All year I've made a big deal of charting our progress toward sales goals set in January. Now it's September, and with a sudden dropoff it's clear we can't possibly make it. How can I handle this without alienating everybody?"

First of all, you don't need to take responsibility for everyone's natural disappointment. Just follow heartpath 2 and let them vent. If you were shortsighted, or the dropoff is in any way attributable to your actions, admit you were wrong via heartpath 10 and then move on to solving the problem: Start by finding a way to acknowledge everyone's efforts so far—heartpath 6—and reward them if you can. Only then should you set new, realistic goals that will keep your salespeople motivated. The worst thing you could do would be to blame them for failure by sticking rigidly to an impossible goal; you, your employees, and your company all lose in this case.

"Two of my most valued employees are polarizing others in the office with their disputes. What can I do?"

If you're a strong communicator who listens with empathy and speaks clearly and passionately (heartpaths 8 and 9), you'll be able to let these two know how you feel and make it safe for them to confide in you even though you might have to say things that one or both will find difficult to hear. Again, first tell them how important they are to the organization; your clarity and passion may motivate them to resolve their differences on their own. Whether you talk to them together or separately and in what way will depend on your empathic reading of what the two personalities need to open their own hearts. A template for high-EQ problem solving is in the next exercise. If you decide one of the two employees must be transferred or let go, use your intuition in choosing between them when practical criteria break out evenly.

It's not unfair to make your decision based on your intuitive feelings about their respective intentions toward you and the organization. Once you've decided, as long as your energy, mental clarity, and regard for others support your choice, don't second-guess it.

"My top salesperson has suddenly stopped performing. What's the best way to approach this problem?"

A low-EQ response would be to cajole, threaten, or otherwise try to manipulate the employee. A high-EQ response would be to follow any hunch that tells you there's a nontransitory problem that requires attention. In that case ask whether something outside work is wrong; see the following exercise. People who have serious personal or other problems often already feel their security threatened, so if you want an honest answer, you'll clear your desk, close your door, and hold all your calls—and your thoughts—while you listen, following heartpaths 2 and 9. In this case expressing sincere concern for the person's well-being might be a better entree than even a positive comment on the touchy subject of performance.

HIGH-EQ PROBLEM SOLVING

It's not easy to approach an employee who is having (or causing) a problem at work in a constructive way. Sometimes you have to ask people to work harder when they are stressed in other parts of their lives, but acknowledging that you understand is encouraging and motivating. Here are general guidelines for preventing defensiveness and creating an open atmosphere for communication.

1. Set aside time when you're not pressured and won't be interrupted; make sure you feel relaxed and emotionally available. Begin with a clear statement such as "Is something troubling you about work?" or "It seems to me that you're on edge [or distracted, disinterested, etc.]" or "I feel very concerned about . . ."

2. Listen to the feelings as well as the words that follow. Be especially alert for changes that signal discomfort or pain—an altered

tempo or tone of voice, change in expression, compulsive behavior such as knuckle cracking or nail biting. Then be prepared for any answer you get. Sometimes managers who anticipate garden-variety complaints about overwork are shocked and paralyzed by the news that substance abuse or another serious problem exists.

3. If your employee seems to be unaware of the problem at work, you may want to gently probe. "Is something going on in another part of your life that could be affecting you at work?" Let the person know nonverbally or with a few words that you heard.

4. Now the two of you are ready to problem-solve. You may ask, "What can you do to change the situation?" "What can I do to make it easier for you at this time?"

"I'm thinking of transferring Melissa. She really gets on my nerves, and I find myself losing my patience with her all the time. I guess it's just a case of personality conflict. What else can I do?"

You're probably asking the question because transferring her doesn't feel right—the idea leaves you feeling tired and small. But that doesn't solve your problem, so you need to find out why you're so mad at this person. Why does she bug you? Why can't you be more tolerant? If you really have no idea, maybe it's time to meet the teacher that bites.

MIRROR, MIRROR: DEALING FAIRLY WITH PEOPLE WHO TRIGGER UNCOMFORTABLE FEELINGS

1. Begin with the Building Emotional Muscle process. Once you're relaxed and have allowed your feelings to intensify, ask yourself the following questions: "Am I feeling resentment, envy, or jealousy?"

2. If any of these questions resonate at all, continue: "If I'm resentful, what am I resentful of? What do I see in this person that

I would like to have?" If it is something you need, you'll be able to redirect your energies to go after it.

Another tack is to ask your feelings, "Is there something about this person that reminds me of a part of myself I don't like?" When we come face to face with a quality or characteristic that we're not completely comfortable with in ourselves, it can seem intolerable in someone else. Review and use the techniques in chapter 4 to rebuild your self-acceptance.

Being a Great Employee Through EQ

Even those who manage other people are usually supervised by someone else, so anyone can take the advice that follows. Being a good employee is mainly a matter of doing what you were hired for while retaining your own integrity. And if you're like most of us, it's also a matter of getting ahead. Here are some ways to do that:

• *When there's a problem, speak up.* It would be great if we all had high-EQ bosses, but even the most empathic boss doesn't have time to ferret out your feelings. Strong physical pangs that won't go away will tell you when you shouldn't stay silent.

• *Know what you want from this job.* If you don't know what you want, you can't ask for it. What's most important to you at this point in your life, and how do you expect this job to fulfill those needs? Use the exploring exercises on pages 180–181 if you've lost touch with your heartfelt job needs.

• *Know how well you're performing from day to day.* The most demoralizing occupational event I know of is to be fired without any idea it was coming. Layoffs aside, it hardly ever has to be that way. If you're keeping your mental powers sharp and you know your job is enhancing your well-being, you're probably performing well and doing what's right for you. As long as you're staying empathic enough to know that it's also right for your boss and the organization, you should never be taken by surprise.

• *Know what your boss feels is important.* This isn't always what he or she *says* is important. Attune to everything that expresses feelings—what the boss does vs. says, where the boss's own fears seem to lie, how the boss treats other people—to get an idea of how to fulfill the boss's needs on the job. With empathy you'll feel an echo of your boss's emotions as long as you're paying attention.

• *Know the values of the organization and how you feel about them.* Every organization has a personality, too. Especially at a new job, keep your eyes, ears, and heart open for information about the organization's M.O. You need to know not just what the organization's production goals are but how it does business. Is it a three-piece-suit atmosphere or a shirtsleeves workplace? Do people chat casually and spontaneously or make appointments with each other? Are plans made openly or secretly? Is the organization's style conservative or daring, people oriented or product oriented? How are people treated when let go? Is hiring done first from within or always from without? Are loyalty and camaraderie in evidence? Do coworkers like each other or merely tolerate each other?

Where do you fit in? Do you like what you discover? If not, what can you live with and what makes you feel physically uncomfortable? Knowing that will help you navigate a successful course for as long as you decide to stay with this organization.

"I'm really unhappy about the way things are going, but my boss is swamped right now. What's the best way to be heard?"
First, be sure it's really a work problem. If it's one that comes from home or elsewhere, follow heartpath 10 and ask for the help you need to cope at work. If it is a work issue, make sure it's really important to you, or you'll be wasting your time and your boss's. Do you take this problem home with you? Is it beginning to affect the rest of your life? If so, you have to speak up (heartpath 8). When you do, begin with something positive to set the stage (heartpath 7).

How well do you know your boss? Under what circumstances is he or she usually most relaxed and receptive? When does the boss schedule meetings that may involve conflicts of interest? How much warning does he or she appreciate? Would you be better off paying close attention and then grabbing your chance when you can, or scheduling an appointment and preceding it with a memo of what you need to discuss? The key is to know what will work best for *both of you* and to make sure your statements are delivered with the passion that will make them compelling. "Getting into Your Boss's Shoes" on the next page can help you exercise your empathy to understand where the boss stands.

"I'd really like more responsibility [or money, benefits, training, etc.], but I know if I ask in the wrong way, the issue will be dead for another year. How can I get what I want?"

Follow the heartpaths described for the preceding question, including using the "Getting into Your Boss's Shoes" exercise. Also, if you know what you want will cause problems—the budget won't allow it, the organizational structure is rigid, your boss will have to spend too much time figuring out the logistics—be prepared to offer solutions or at least approaches to getting there. Show that you know how your request will affect everyone else in the organization and that you're willing to be flexible to achieve your goals. Can you tactfully ask the boss how he or she feels about your request? Via heartpath 5 you can offer to compromise or take a wait-and-see attitude. Can you take heartpath 6 and be prepared to yield something to avoid stepping on a coworker's toes? Whatever you offer as evidence that you need what you're after, be sure it includes heartfelt conviction, not just numbers.

"I'm really in over my head and I need help, but I'm afraid asking for it will be a sign that I'm not up to this job. What should I do?"

First, use your ability to gauge the intensity of your feelings to determine how urgent the problem is. If you feel only moderately anxious, quickly imagine various solutions. If none of them makes you feel at ease again, whether you can afford to wait out the problem for a while depends on your intuitive feeling about the seriousness of the problem. If you can't sleep at night and you're getting a strong hunch that disaster is approaching, don't delay: Follow heartpath 10 and ask for the help you need. Your boss is likely to appreciate your willingness to admit imperfection in the name of protecting the organization's interests.

"I love my job, but I can't stand my boss. I don't want to be forced to leave because of one person. What can I do?"

If you've been using your EQ skills to try to understand your boss and you're still at loggerheads, try the following exercise. It's a potent way of connecting empathically and may help break down any stubborn barriers.

GETTING INTO YOUR BOSS'S SHOES

This is a role-playing exercise involving an imaginary conversation with your boss.

1. Begin by telling your boss what's troubling you. Use "I feel" messages to get your points across.

2. Now change position or take another chair and imagine that you are your boss, who has just listened to what you said. Get into the boss's character, shoes, body. What does your boss feel? How does he or she respond?

3. Go back and forth, moving each time you change roles and doing your best to get into character, until you're as familiar with your boss's feelings and needs as with your own.

4. Now go ahead and have a talk with your boss if you feel it's appropriate.

Being a Great Coworker Through EQ

Being a good coworker is largely a matter of contributing to the esprit de corps. It might seem preferable to stick to yourself and just get your job done, but people who try that tack inevitably discover that their own interests as well as those of the organization suffer as a result. Unfortunately, cultivating good relationships with your fellow employees can be a challenge. Not everyone will view you as a comrade, and you in turn won't feel open and trust-ing around everyone you work with. Your intuition about people is indispensable in such cases. Here are a few ways to use it to your advantage:

• *Don't make assumptions about those you work with.* It's so easy to make your workplace a microcosm for the prejudices with which you approach the world. You may not have to get to know your coworkers as well as your boss or employees, but you'll never learn anything about them if you begin by assuming that recent college grads are always arrogant or almost-retireds are stodgy; that women can be manipulated by emotions and men by data. Let your emotions show you what's unique about everyone.

• *Don't expect anyone to communicate with 100 percent hon-esty.* Some people seem incapable of plain speaking at work. They're afraid, they're too polite, they're cautious, and they rarely say what they mean or mean what they say. You can wait until you've been burned several times to figure it out, or you can pay extra attention to what your body tells you they feel, and less to what they say. Trust your intuition about people. Be par-ticularly alert with people who may view you as a competitor.

• *Be prepared to draw the line.* Heartpath 3 suggests that there's a limit to how close you'll want to be with a coworker, but that doesn't mean you won't or shouldn't form friendships at work. If you share the values and goals of the organization and its other employees, there's a good chance that you'll find friends there. Stay acutely attuned to your own feelings, however, so you know when you want to be an acquaintance, not a close friend. Don't let emotional blackmail or office politics pressure you into relationships you don't want. If you feel uneasy with a relation-ship, trust your hunch and back off. If a work conflict comes up with someone who is now a close friend, you'll be able to tell from the intensity of your own feelings and your empathic feel-ings where your priorities lie.

• *Offer help; don't wait for people to ask.* Not only will your generosity contribute to the esprit de corps, but your sensitivity to the needs of others will gain you their future support and loyalty.

• *Don't take it personally.* Remember that everyone has an agenda, a personal life (fraught with problems), and a unique style of interaction. You don't have to take anyone's behavior personally. Let coworkers' behavior bring out your empathy, not your sympathy (see chapter 6). You can understand how they might be feeling without being consumed by emotional memory or taking responsibility for their angst. Let it slide and follow heartpath 6 when you can.

"I know Doug is padding his expense account, leaving early when the boss isn't looking, and generally getting away with murder. Should I say something?"

How strongly do you feel about it? You don't have to turn to ethics, rules, or morals to answer that question but to how much the issue bothers you—follow heartpath 8. People whose EQ is new usually take on everyone who bugs them, because they're not yet familiar with the subtle ranges of feeling. Most feelings seem strong and therefore compel them to act. Once you've been using EQ for a while, you'll realize that you don't have to champion every cause that comes your way. Use the Building Emotional Muscle process to imagine how you'll feel if you do and if you don't say anything; try out the possibilities of talking to Doug directly and of talking to someone in a position of power.

"I've come up with a great way to save on overhead, which will make me a shoo-in for a promotion, but it will mean cutbacks in Ann's department. How can I handle this?"

Only you can decide how you'll feel about any action you take. Why not talk to Ann, following heartpaths 2 and 9, to find out exactly how she'll feel about this? Attuning empathically to her reaction while staying in touch with your own feelings will help you decide whether or not you can and should follow heartpath 6 and put your needs second. If your relationship is good, you can use your two heads and hearts to come up with a solution that will serve you both—and the company you work for.

"Our managers have asked John and me to work together to come up with a new computer system for the office, but he won't share his research, and I found out he actually gave me some out-of-date figures the other day. Why won't he cooperate?"

As I've said, many people in the workplace are so afraid that their position is tenuous that they see cooperation as a threat to their own security. Empathizing with John's fear might persuade you to take extra measures to dispel his fear: Are there places where you could follow heartpath 8 and yield to his wishes? Can you invest extra effort into following heartpaths 2 and 9? Can you make a point of rejecting a major opportunity to take advantage of John, thereby proving yourself a nonthreat? If these measures are ineffective, and you consistently get a strong negative feeling from John, pay attention to it and protect yourself. If working with someone else isn't an option, keep your distance as well as you can, which may mean accepting that you'll have to do the work of two people on your own. If John continues to be uncooperative but you feel no malice from him, try the following technique.

SUCCESSFULLY NEGOTIATING A PROBLEM WITH A COWORKER

The point of this exercise is to overcome fear of confrontation and initiate communication with a coworker—it is not about changing anyone. Remember, the most powerful and lasting tool we have for influencing others is heartfelt communication.

1. Follow the instructions for the beginning and middle parts of the Building Emotional Muscle exercise.

2. Use as your point of focus the feeling you experience as you imagine yourself confronting a coworker about a problem you are having with him or her.

3. Work with Building Emotional Muscle until feelings of fear no longer intimidate you.

4. Now set the stage for a successful dialogue by arranging to meet in a relaxed informal setting—lunchtime or after work somewhere. Because the problem is yours, you may have to go further out of your way to accommodate the other person's time constraints.

5. Own the problem as yours, because it is even if it involves this other person. Send a short, clear, positive message about what you would like. For example: "I would like your help, cooperation, friendship," and send the message with heart as well as head.

6. Listen with empathy to the response and ask again if you feel the person didn't hear you. Don't expect him or her to agree with you. If you feel that you've communicated your message clearly, you've done all you can. Leave it at that.

The ball is now in your coworker's court, and it's up to him or her to take action. Going to management is always a fallback position but one made stronger by your effort to solve the problem.

"There are people at the office I would like to be more friendly with, but I have difficulty reaching out. How can I make some friends here?"

Here is a helpful exercise for shy people.

REACHING OUT FOR FRIENDS AT WORK

Do this exercise before you fall asleep at night and when you wake in the morning.

1. Use the Building Emotional Muscle exercise to relax and focus.

2. Imagine yourself reaching out to others. By this I mean see, hear, touch, taste, smell, and above all feel the scenario you create. Perhaps you have someone particular in mind. Create a scenario that includes your shy feelings in the process but permits you to go beyond them.

3. The next day, follow through on your friendly intentions and remember to breathe deeply just as you did in the planning exercise.

WHEN HIGH EQ MEETS LOW EQ IN THE WORKPLACE

Here are some suggestions for responding to seemingly intractable individuals in a high-EQ manner.

"My bosses have no idea what they're doing. What should I do?"
If you like your job, if you believe in what the organization is doing, one option is to help them do their job better. If they don't appreciate your support and reward you accordingly, you may want to look elsewhere, but if they value you, as well they might, your future may be bright. Many people find real satisfaction in knowing that their behind-the-scenes work permits a person or an organization to flourish.

"The people I work with are completely unappreciative. They never say thank you, they act like they're doing me a big favor when I ask for something, though I do *them* favors all the time, and they notice me only when I've done something wrong. Should I put up with this?"
Start with yourself. Do you feel you're doing a good job? If so, why? Make a list and put it up someplace where you'll see it frequently. If you feel confident about your value, approval will be less important to you. From a position of confidence, it will also be easier to take an unappreciative person aside and say how discouraged you feel. Whether or not they end up changing, knowing that you've acted to get what you want enhances your self-esteem.

A Paradigm for Working Smart

Remember Hank and Sally from chapter 7? Hank started out as a computer programmer. Enjoying the technical part of his job but finding his coworkers hard to reach, he set up a lunchtime bridge tournament and soon a third of the people in his section were getting together regularly. Hank's boss noted his ability to bring people together and asked Hank to interface with a difficult big customer.

Sally's first job was selling cosmetics at a department store. It was intellectually unchallenging, but Sally found it rewarding to help the older women use makeup successfully and collected a loyal following of customers. Sally accepted her manager's offer of a chance to sell in other departments and ended up selling successfully in every department and training other employees. Still, she missed the interaction with the customers she felt needed her.

A promotion to management in his thirties brought Hank more money, but he missed the technical challenges. A talk with his boss resulted in a new job—technical troubleshooter. "Better," he told Sally, "but now all I do is fix other people's mistakes."

Bored by her sales work, Sally decided to go back to school. Knowing she loved work that helped people, she followed a hunch and decided to retrain as a social worker. She loved the training and brought to it her experiences in the home and work setting. With her sales background, she landed a job as assistant director of a small social service agency, where she became the outside person in charge of marketing and fund-raising.

As soon as Sally was settled in her new job, Hank cut the cord with his old company and returned to school to retrain as an architectural engineer, a job that would allow him to use his technical skills creatively, make his own mistakes, and put him in contact with others. Though he was older than the competition, Hank's enthusiasm got him a great job.

Within five years, Sally was heading the agency she'd started with and had grown her staff from ten to nearly forty. Sally balanced the needs of clients, staff, and her board of directors by making sure she stayed relaxed and in touch with the feelings of hope and usefulness that kept her motivated. She meditated briefly before breakfast each morning, bicycled back and forth to work or picked up a game of indoor tennis after work, and knew where her priorities lay at all times by staying in touch with her feelings. When an earthquake damaged the housing of her homeless clients, it also damaged the office. She and her staff had to double up for eight months, but the atmosphere of flexibility Sally had encouraged at the office allowed them all to adapt, and they still managed to keep the agency on track. Knowing that as a leader she set an example that others would follow, she worked hardest on herself to remain relaxed, hopeful, and caring. People followed her lead and laughed at the inconveniences all shared. "This tragedy has brought the staff and me closer than ever," she told Hank.

Hank's ability to keep clients happy made him a highly valued member of his firm, and at age fifty he was made a partner. This position gave him the opportunity to use the company resources in behalf of projects that supported his community values. And a byproduct has been more customers for the firm. Hank now vows to continue working as long as he can. "I'll never retire," he recently told Sally. "I may change jobs, or work without being paid, but I want to give myself to some sort of work as long as I can."

Sally took her bout with cancer as a wake-up call that she needed more time for herself. She retired from the agency and spent time exploring interests that she had put on the back burner, like yoga, art, and meditation retreats. Within six months, however, she know she had lost something important— the excitement and challenge of feeling needed and useful. To satisfy these needs, she began working as a consultant and offered her services free to nonprofit groups she admired. Sally attributes the fact that she remains cancer-free, healthy, and excited about life to the deep satisfaction she now feels.

9

The High EQ at Home

There's nothing like family.

The people we're related to by blood and marriage should be our closest allies, our greatest sources of love and support. Too often, however, our interactions with them are filled with misunderstanding and resentment, bickering and badgering. Those we should know and be known by best end up feeling like strangers.

Usually that's because emotional consciousness is an on-again, off-again state. Sometimes we really open ourselves to our families—we don't just give them a verbal rundown of what's new in our lives, but show them our deepest feelings—and we discover the profound joy of mutual understanding. At other times we let old hurts and gripes intrude on current interaction, and any hope we have of staying close as everyone changes and grows evaporates. Family is where our first and strongest emotional memories are made, and that's where they keep cropping up.

This is why EQ succeeds where other efforts at family harmony fail. Active awareness and empathy—the ability to be aware, accepting, and permanently attuned to ourselves and others—tells us how to respond to one another's needs.

EQ is incredibly powerful in the family because it puts *you* in control of your relationships with parents and children, siblings and in-laws. When you know how you feel, you can't be manipulated by others' emotions; nor can you blame family strife on

everyone else. Most of the techniques for improving family relationships in this chapter are therefore centered on communicating your feelings to those you care about.

First and foremost, close relationships are centered around
feeling. Without emotional exchange, family contact becomes a
burden, because no one is comfortable spending that much time
with strangers. So if you want your family members to know and
accept each other lovingly, you have to begin with your own
emotional honesty and openness. When you do, the suggestions
offered here are transformed from familiar reasonable advice to
highly effective methods for bringing your family ever closer.
Let's start with some basic rules of thumb.

• *Look to yourself first.* A family is a system made up of inter-
dependent individuals, but that doesn't mean you can blame your
family of origin for the way you are today, any more than you can
hold your mate and children responsible for your personal happiness. Your best hope for fixing any family problem is to attend
to your own emotional health. Emotional awareness will give you
the fortitude to resist emotional blackmail and to provide for
your own needs even in the face of strident demands from loved
ones. When you act on the conviction that you have a right and
obligation to assert your own emotional needs, your family will
notice that your emotional independence benefits not only you
but the whole family, and they may quickly follow your lead.

• *Remember that consistency builds trust.* Studies have shown
that lack of consistency destroys trust. Intermittent emotional
awareness will cause those who love and depend on you, especially children, to get confused and frightened. That's why it's so
important to keep your awareness active with family. When you
feel yourself disconnecting, do the remedial work suggested in
chapter 5 (page 111).

• *Recognize that being close doesn't mean being clones.* Sometimes family ties blind us to the uniqueness of those we love.
Pride in the family continuum can make it easy to forget that

Mary can't be expected to have the same talents as Molly, even though they do look a lot alike; that Joe Junior won't necessarily choose to follow in Joe Senior's footsteps; or that you and I should spend our leisure time joined at the hip just because we're married.

If you've done your work in chapters 5 and 6, however, you should already be gaining profound insight into your loved ones without confusing your feelings with theirs. In action, this enlightenment translates into honoring and celebrating differences and offering what each person needs, not what *you* would need in their circumstances.

• *Remember that knowing people all your life doesn't mean understanding them.* "I knew you when . . ." doesn't mean I know you now, no matter how much I've always loved you. We all change, and yet each of us seems to see change only in ourselves. How infuriating it is to be introduced as someone's kid brother when you're fifty-five or to be perpetually treated as the airhead you were at fourteen despite the fact that you're now CEO of your own company. Now that you've acquired empathy, you can gently steer your family away from stagnant patterns of interaction by modeling the feeling attention you'd like to receive. When you're with your family, don't automatically seek the conversational refuge of talking over old times. Ask what's new and show that you really care by eliciting details and then listening with your body as well as your mind.

• *Watch out for destructive emotional memories.* Catching your thirty-year-old self responding to a parent in the voice of the five-year-old you can make you feel weak and frustrated. With EQ you don't need to keep getting snared by emotional memories. Whenever you feel out of control with family— whether it's kicking yourself for acting like a five-year-old with your parents or agonizing over where the anger you're dumping on your innocent spouse and children is coming from—return to Building Emotional Muscle Part II to explore the memories that are imposing on your behavior today.

• *Cherish every stage of life in each family member.* No matter how well we understand intellectually that it can't happen, we desperately want Mom and Dad to stay the way they are and the kids to stay at home forever. The best way I know to accept that fact emotionally is to *embrace* change. Accept the natural fear that your parents' aging evokes, but use your emotional awareness and empathy to figure out how you can cherish this moment for its unique qualities. What can you and your parents' share now that wasn't possible in the past? Can you keep having fun and make sure everyone still feels useful and worthy in the family support system even though roles and responsibilities must be altered?

If you're not sure what will work, ask. Fully accepting your fear of change can make it easier to broach subjects that you may have considered awkward in the past. Maybe your parents are just waiting for your cue. Feel them out!

In a flexible, healthy family dynamic, change is just one of the many opportunities you have to enrich one another. The following ten paths will lead you to many others.

HeartPaths: 10 Ways to Live Smart with Your Family

1. *Take care of your health if you hope to take care of anyone else.* The more demanding of your time your family is, the more you need to fit in exercise. Perhaps you and your family can seek out ways to exercise together.

2. *Listen if you expect to be heard.* Lack of communication is the loudest complaint in most families. The answer to "Why won't they listen to me?" may be simply "You're not listening to them."

3. *Teach emotional choice.* Manage your moods by letting all feelings be OK, but *not* all behaviors. Model behavior that respects and encourages the feelings and rights of others yet makes it clear we have a choice about what to do with what we feel.

4. *Teach generosity by receiving as well as giving.* Giving and receiving are parts of the same loving continuum. If we don't give, we find it hard to receive, and if we can't receive, we don't really have much to give. This is why selflessness carried to extremes is of little benefit to others.

5. *Take responsibility for what you communicate silently.* The very young and old are especially sensitive to nonverbal cues. More than our words, tone of voice, posture (body language), and facial expressions convey our feelings. We have to listen to our tone of voice and look at ourselves in pictures and in the mirror to assess our emotional congruency. Loving words coming through clenched teeth don't feel loving—they feel confusing.

6. *Don't try to solve problems for your loved ones.* Caring for your family doesn't mean taking charge of their problems, giving unsolicited advice, or protecting them from their own emotions. Let them know their own strengths and allow them to ask you for what they need.

7. *Make a lasting impression through actions.* Your values will be communicated by your actions, no matter what you say. Be an example, not a nag.

8. *Acknowledge your errors to everyone, including younger family members.* Saying you're sorry when you hurt someone you love models humility and emotional integrity. You can demonstrate that no one is perfect but everyone can learn at any age. Apologizing proves you can forgive yourself and makes it easier to forgive others.

9. *Discover what each person's unique needs are.* You can't assume that your grandmother needs the same signs of love as your three-year-old or that either one will have the same needs next year. When in doubt, ask!

10. *Be generous in expressing love.* Everyone in a family (especially young children) needs the emotional reassurance of loving words, gestures, and looks. Those who demand the least emotional attention may need it the most.

High-EQ Parenthood

If you and your mate treat each other and the kids with emotional awareness and empathy, scientists have learned, your children are not too likely to need this book when they grow up. In fact, I'd say instilling respect for emotion is the most important childrearing task you have. Here are a few ways to thwart low-EQ parenting practices:

• *Remember that you can't impart what you don't exemplify.* Your children learn from you—through your actions, via heart-path 7, much more than your words. If you can't communicate your emotions through your behavior, they won't respect their own emotions.

• *Try to learn from your children.* Children haven't unlearned EQ as you have (see chapters 2 and 3 for the reasons and the research). They make friends easily and retain their capacity for joy because they're naturally empathic and instinctively ready to feel their emotions fully and then let them go. So listen and learn; you'll raise your own EQ and instill flexibility and mutual respect into the family.

• *Be on the lookout for repeating history.* It's a lot easier to instill fear of feelings in children than you think, even if you try hard not to. Pick out the parental refrains you identified as most hurtful in the "Home Is Where the Heart Is—Or Is It?" exercise on page 28 of chapter 2 and memorize them—you might even jot them on a piece of paper and put it in your wallet as a way of symbolically keeping them in your memory. When you're tired and irritable, pull out that list and note your own feelings as you read it. This reminder should keep you from shrugging off the warning feelings that arise when you start to utter these refrains yourself. Also, whenever you get a physical signal that you're belittling your child's feelings, do what you can to observe your tone of voice, facial expressions, and body language—run to a mirror if you can. If what you find hurts *you,* it's also hurting your child. You may need to use Building Emotional Muscle periodically to recall how *you* felt being the object of those words and expressions. Invoking those painful experiences is a strong deterrent to repeating history.

Let's be realistic, though; you *will* let your guard down from time to time—we all do. Fortunately, you have at your disposal a simple tool for ensuring that your errors don't do permanent damage. It's called an apology, and it comes in pretty handy throughout parenthood.

• *Remember that unhappy parents raise unhappy children.* If you're exhausted and depressed by the demands of parenthood, your children will be depressed, too. You can't sacrifice yourself and do anyone else any good, so follow heartpath 1 and keep yourself healthy if you hope to raise healthy children.

Using Your Own EQ to Raise High-EQ Children

There will always be a market for another parenting book, because no one can reduce the complexities of rearing children, each one unique, to a list of simple rules. Through astute emotional awareness and empathy, you'll find the correct things to say and do with your child at any given moment. That said, there *are* situations that arise in virtually every childhood, from infancy to puberty, that challenge parents' ability to affirm the worthiness of children's feelings without being manipulated by them. And there are ways to incorporate the tenets of emotional intelligence into your responses to these situations. So I offer the following only as a few examples; I hope that you'll apply the high-EQ approaches illustrated to all the unique challenges that arise in your own parenting adventure.

Fear of the dark. Here's a typical power play that leaves EQ-challenged adults feeling manipulated, guilty, and just plain pooped. Has your child managed to secure a permanent spot in your bed because you can't stand to hear him cry, you remember how afraid you were of the dark at his age, or you're just plain tired of resisting? Assuming you don't want him in your bed at night, your high-EQ alternatives are to empathize (not sympathize) with the child's fear and problem-solve together to come up with a solution that will suit you both: a night light? a change of room? moving the child's bed to a part of the room that feels safer or is naturally brighter? How about a schedule that reduces the time spent in your bed night by night? When your urge to protect is overwhelming, stay on heartpath 6 and err on the side of assuming the child can handle his own feelings. He's not going to die of fear!

Bossiness. When sweet little Allison starts acting like a thug as so many children do at some point, the low-EQ response is to tell her she's doing something wrong (heartpath 7). No matter what words you use, she won't hear you. The high-EQ way is to let her make her own mistakes and learn from them, but if that doesn't feel active enough to you, you can also try saying, without rancor, something like "I don't like it when someone talks to me that way." Also watch for times to engage her empathy when someone else is being bossy and ask, "How do you think that makes the other little girl feel?"

Temper tantrums. I bet you know this one, because it's been in every parenting manual: Ignore these episodes completely. That's a high-EQ response because it sends the message that you refuse to be manipulated by your child's upset. Children who get a response when they throw a tantrum grow up to be bullies.

Greed. Sometimes kids seem to want *everything* they see, including things they don't need and won't use. Tell them that greed is sinful and shameful and they'll feel evil and ashamed— and you'll never know what emptiness they were trying to fill. The high-EQ response comes from heartpath 9: Ask yourselves, "Are we loving this child the way the child needs to be loved?"

Staring. We're usually in such a hurry to stop this behavior before it offends the person being stared at that we confuse children about their feelings. Don't hustle them off, distract them, or chastise them. Instead, acknowledge their natural fascination with those who are different from the children by saying something like "I know, that bothers me, too. What must it feel like to have to live on the street (or be in a wheelchair, or

have scars like that, etc.)?" Then help your children understand that when our empathy is evoked we act on it: "This is
what we can do to help . . ."

Childhood myths. People who are ruled by their own needs
regarding these fantasies always end up going to extremes, being
brutally matter-of-fact about the tooth fairy and Santa Claus or
going to absurd lengths to perpetuate these myths. The child's
needs should always rule here. Fantasy has to do with hope, and
if a myth seems emotionally important to the child's outlook,
you don't have to burst the child's bubble in the name of honesty. Nor do you have to lie; by conveying the idea that belief
and faith are personal qualities, you let the child decide when
to let go.

Learning as You Go: Using EQ to Handle Change in Childhood

In chapter 5 I told you to be on the lookout for crises that disconnect you from emotional awareness. Looking at it pessimisti-
cally, you might view parenthood as one long crisis. Taking the
optimistic tack, you can anticipate certain points in parenthood
as challenges that measure your emotional mettle. Not surprisingly, the first is new parenthood.

"I'm so tired I'm numb; so lonely that I'm always irritable and out of touch with the world."

When you're a brand-new parent, you have to guard against
giving so much at first that you end up with nothing left to give
at all. The solution is to follow heartpaths 1 and 4 from the start:
Take care of yourself and ask for or accept help when you need
it. Sleep may seem like the obvious answer if you're exhausted,
but that may not be what you need to replenish you. Use the
Building Emotional Muscle exercise to recall what has truly
relaxed, renewed, and reenergized you in the past: Having time
alone to read, draw, listen to music, or pursue a hobby? Going to
a party, gardening, or sitting around with friends? Then be sure
to get the help you need to make time for those activities.

- Reach out to everyone you know with "I feel" messages that express your needs.
- Find other parents who may be interested in a baby-sitting exchange.
- Make use of community facilities such as the Y, churches, or synagogues.
- Call family service agencies listed in the Yellow Pages for help in hooking up with supportive resources.

It's crucial to find someone to talk to about your feelings about new parenthood, especially if you're a single parent. High-EQ parents look for a way to ease their fears about their new role rather than deny them, and a support group can be just the ticket. When you tell the truth about your frustrated and angry feelings and fantasies, your loving feelings for your children will bubble up, and you'll go back to your caretaker role more refreshed and loving.

Finally—and maybe most important—keep your sense of humor. If you can learn to laugh at your ineptitude as a new parent, your fears won't overwhelm you. You'll remain intellectually open to the myriad ways to raise kids successfully. Check the humor section of your local bookstore; there are always (surprise, surprise) a number of hilarious new sendups on parenthood. Or watch a couple of TV cartoons—you might as well get used to it.

"My wife and I are pretty outgoing and confident, and our daughter is a lot like us, but our son seems so withdrawn. Is something wrong with him?"

We all strut like the proudest peacocks once we get through our firstborn's infancy—and then comes child number two and a whole new ballgame. Fortunately, your EQ can fill in when everything you learned about your first child fails to reveal anything about your second.

Because our feelings help us understand each individual, emotionally aware and accepting parents pick up on the strengths and weaknesses peculiar to each child and can appreciate and accommodate these differences (heartpath 9). If you're stumped about how to interact with your son because he's not that much like you, look to his sister for an empathy lesson. When they're both rested and relaxed, your young daughter will show that she understands and accepts their personality differences by playing quietly with her little brother. You too can be playful with the boisterous child and quietly attentive to the introspective one. Remember, too, that children who are shy or withdrawn may need more of your time. You might read interactively with your son or join him in imaginary games as he plays in the bathtub, using these opportunities to talk about your feelings and his.

"The kids quarrel and fight with one another, and it drives me crazy. Don't they love each other?"

This is another example of the exponentially greater challenges that a second child brings into a family. Were you shocked and ashamed of your three-year-old when she greeted her new baby brother by telling him to go back to the hospital and then hitting him? Sibling rivalry is a classic example of the need to separate acceptable feelings from unacceptable behavior; remember heartpath 3. Whenever you see the slightest sign of rivalry on the part of your daughter, reassure her that you understand her feelings. (And make sure you do. Having a new sibling show up would be like having your husband bring home a new, younger wife one day and expect you to put up with it.) Then reiterate that she may not hurt the baby. Parent manuals are full of good ideas for handling this problem; again, the important thing is that the feelings are perfectly all right while the actions might not be (heartpath 3).

When you teach kids to accept their feelings by listening and acknowledging them via heartpath 2, take responsibility for what you communicate nonverbally (heartpath 5), and follow heartpath 10 in expressing your love copiously, you provide your children with an emotionally supportive environment. High EQ builds emotional security in each child and, consequently, caring and respect among siblings. The answer to the next question applies, too.

"My son lies to me and sometimes takes things that don't belong to him; my daughter disobeys me. Sometimes they don't seem to have any morals at all. What are we doing wrong?"

By pointing out the difference between feelings that are OK and hurtful actions that are not—heartpath 3—you teach the difference between what we feel and the way we behave. The trick here is to be aware of the emotional messages you send at such times, so watch your nonverbal as well as verbal communications (heartpath 5). The fondest wish of most young children is to gain your approval, so lies and rebellion may be their ways of expressing confusion about what you expect. If you're angry and judgmental, the offending child will likely focus on his or her feelings toward you rather than toward the actual transgression.

The high-EQ approach, therefore, is to engage the child's empathy by giving the child the opportunity to experience what it feels like to have hurt another: "I bet you really wanted that truck and got mad when you couldn't have it. I'd probably feel that way, too, but how would you feel if someone took *your* favorite truck?" The low-EQ approach, to instill shame in the child, only guarantees that if the child has the nerve to try stealing again, you'll never know about it.

To be the level-headed, compassionate, and loving disciplinarian you want to be, you have to manage your own feelings of frustration. The following exercises can help.

TIME OUT FOR MOM OR DAD

This is a variation on "Getting a Grip on a Crazed Amygdala" in chapter 7 (page 167). Try both versions and see which works best for you. If you're alone with your children and your amygdala is about to blow:

1. Put your children in a place where they can't hurt themselves—a crib for an infant, or at a neighbor's for a few minutes.

Treat this situation like an emergency—which it is if you've experienced abuse as a child.

2. Take a shower and/or a series of full deep breaths—stay out of your head and in your body.

3. Sit down (a rocking chair is soothing) and focus on the physical experiences in your body as you did when you practiced Building Emotional Muscle.

4. Breathe into your feelings until you feel in charge of yourself.

5. Some people enjoy imagining that they're being held, cradled and comforted by a loving protective caretaker.

TAKING YOUR TROUBLES TO A LISTENING HEART

Find someone who will agree to let you call and emote for four or five minutes whenever you feel frazzled by parenting. Because you don't want advice, but just want to be heard, an acquaintance may be the best choice, but a friend or family member who can avoid interfering is also fine. Not everyone is willing and able to do this, but those who are might appreciate your offer to do the same for them in exchange.

When you make a call, it's OK if you run out of steam before four or five minutes are up. Just keep expressing your feelings without interruption until you feel satiated.

Emotional Intelligence with Adolescents

Adolescence creates difficulties for many families, because no one knows how to weather the enormous changes that teenagers are going through. Children naturally pull away from you as they pass into adulthood, but you'll be hard-pressed to see that they get there safe and whole if you disconnect from your emotions. You'll need all your empathy to remain understanding when hormonal upheaval turns your adorable kids into unpredictable, irritable rebels. It also takes sharp active awareness to remain the source of security and wisdom that your teenagers need more than ever before.

You can maintain a sense of balance even when adolescence seems to turn your world upside down, as long as you've cemented your emotional connection with your children throughout their younger years. Mutual respect, loving acceptance of the inevitable changes that families undergo, and a stalwart sense of humor will go a long way toward preventing injurious rifts. Here are a few high-EQ tips:

• *Give young teenagers a job or two that they can do well.* Actually, this is a habit you should begin earlier in childhood, but for preteens it's essential. If they are to become independent and autonomous, they must have a strong sense of self-worth, which you can instill by relying on them in some tangible way. When watching your children evokes a sense of energetic satisfaction in you, stop and pay close attention to what they're doing. Your feelings are probably empathic and will tell you what activities positively energize your teens. Then you can tap those to assign significant chores or tasks.

• *Don't get too hooked on being liked.* If it's important to you that your kids think you're a cool parent, you're answering your needs, not theirs. You need to be able to allow them to assert themselves in ways that don't impinge on the rest of the family's needs and rights, even if it means seeming to reject you. Don't let your hurt dominate your decisions. That's quite a balancing act, one that EQ can help you achieve through empathy and active awareness. If you find yourself repeatedly feeling hurt, ask yourself if those feelings are blocking awareness of your teen's feelings. If you find yourself constantly bending over backward to accommodate your child, take time to review what *you* need.

• *Always apologize when you've been wrong, even in small ways.* Apologizing when you've made a mistake shows your teenagers that you respect them as maturing people, assuages adolescent fear of appearing awkward or foolish by modeling acceptance of our foibles, and prevents resentments from piling up between you.

• *Above all, be generous with your love.* You can take responsibility for the buttons teenagers press in you and continue to let them know that you love them—heartpath 10—even though you won't permit them to do all the things they may want to do. In high-EQ homes frogs eventually turn back into princes and princesses—but you have to kiss them first!

High-EQ Answers to Complaints About Teenagers

"My son dyed his hair green on one side and red on the other" . . . "My daughter thinks *I'm* foolish" . . . "My son is disrespectful and rude to everyone" . . . "My daughter pretends she doesn't know us" . . . "We find cigarette butts and junk food wrappers in his room" . . . "She talks constantly on the phone, and it's interfering with her schoolwork."

If you have a teenager at home, you know why I lumped all those complaints together: all teenagers may very well commit all of these infractions before they're through with you. The good news is that these seemingly rebellious activities are irritating but completely normal and, with the exception of cigarette smoking, basically healthy. You should probably be more concerned about the teenager who is a goody two-shoes; he or she may be afraid to tell you about feeling depressed. Are you following heartpath 2 and listening with all your heart?

At least when teenagers act out under your nose, you're there to love, guide, and model high EQ. You can set an example of respect for your body through heartpath 1, teach emotional choice (heartpath 3), and model the behaviors you value through your actions and deeds through heartpath 7. You can create agreements for ensuring that time on the phone doesn't replace homework. You can listen with empathy, even when you don't like the words, and send clear "I feel" messages when you set limits.

"I'm afraid I'm going to lose my teenager. I have no control over her anymore" . . . "I don't care for his new friends at all" . . . "I don't think I can trust her—I've caught her lying too often."

Low-EQ parents *have* lost their teenagers, usually by alternately overreacting and underreacting. The active awareness described in chapter 5 will allow you to distinguish obnoxious from destructive behavior. It will also keep you from minimizing threats and leaving them vulnerable to danger.

Watch out for knee-jerk reactions to kids you don't like. Before you call your child's friends a bad influence, be sure you're not just jealous of their closeness with your child. If your feelings tell you they really are dangerous, tell your teenager how you feel and what your worries are.

Sometimes the best way to reach a child you're worried about is to find an adult confidant—a relative, close friend, teacher—to take your place for the time being. If the fact that you can't fill that role right now hurts, remind yourself that your child's rejection is part of his or her need for autonomy and use Building Emotional Muscle to imagine how you'll feel knowing your child has someone to confide in compared to how you feel right now, with the child adrift.

Here's another idea: My good friend and next-door neighbor and I agreed to exchange "impossible" fourteen-year-olds one summer, and both daughters gladly returned home after a couple of weeks, having realized that the grass wasn't greener on the other side of the fence. While their adolescent behavior didn't actually improve much, the important result was that their parents' feelings about it did!

Here are a few more ideas for getting heartfelt communication going between you and your teenagers again.

• *Understand why your buttons get pushed.* You can't hope to get close again if just being near each other sets off sparks. Use the Building Emotional Muscle process to relax deeply and focus on the intense feelings that flare up repeatedly with your teenagers. Allow the feelings to intensify as you ask yourself whether these are old feelings and what their nature is—anger, hurt, shame, fear? Most hot buttons exist thanks to emotional memories, so this exercise can tell you whether the flare-ups are caused by your teenager's behavior or some old memory. If the latter, you should now be able to control yourself better with your child.

• *Put yourself in your teenager's shoes.* Before you decide to ask your teenager to change some behavior that bothers you, use the "Getting into Your Boss's Shoes" exercise from the last chapter to imagine the dialogue you'll have. Assuming your child's body language and facial expressions so that you fully understand the child's mood, imagine the child's emotional response to your request. If you imagine the child becoming upset, what does the child find threatening, embarrassing, or difficult about the subject? In other words, how does the child feel, and how does this explain the child's bothersome behavior? The empathic insight you gain from this exercise greatly improves your chances of getting through to your adolescent.

• *Find out what you need from each other.* Directly stating your interest in knowing what your child needs is another way to use empathy to bring you back together. Whether your focus is a specific bone of contention or the whole animal, you can negotiate with an adolescent in a mutually loving and respectful way by having each of you make a list of three to five things you need from each other. Then make a list of the things you each think the other needs from you. Exchange lists, compare, and determine what each of you is willing to give, what exchanges you might make.

Using EQ to Get Along with Adult Relatives

Two elements threaten harmonious relations with parents and adult siblings, in-laws and adult children: lack of time and an abundance of emotional memories. The two add up to the fear that we'll be overwhelmed by each other's needs, giving up ourselves if we give anything to these adult relatives. We do need to invest time in figuring out what our parents want most from us, sustaining close friendships with brothers and sisters, and gathering together without fulfilling every bad joke ever written about contentious, selfish families. But EQ gives us so much energy and creativity that the demands of these relationships need not be onerous. We recognize change as it occurs in individuals and relationships, and we can control our emotional reactions by recognizing emotional memories when they're triggered. Keep your EQ strong, and your adult family encounters are no longer dominated by cleaning up after mistakes and managing crises that have already wreaked havoc.

You and Your Adult Children

Many parents are dismayed to find that they can't just sit back and enjoy the fruits of their labor once they've successfully ushered their children into adulthood. No relationship stands still. The key to a successful ongoing relationship with your grown children is your ability to deal with the change and growth that presage role reversal. *You* have to keep the lines of emotional communication open; your children may be wrapped up in career, love, and friendships at this stage in their lives. Let them know how you feel and what you need from them.

If you've only recently raised your EQ, of course, you may have some amending to do, some changes to make in your style of interaction with your children. Do they avoid you because you force advice or your own choices on them? Do you bring more disappointment and judgment to the relationship than they can tolerate? Have you followed heartpath 2 and listened empathically to how your children feel about their choices? How about heartpath 9—have you tried to find out what their unique needs are? Some adult children keep their distance because they feel injured by past experiences with you; in that case the only way to improve the relationship is to stick to heartpaths 2 and 8—listen to their hurt and then admit you were wrong. Here are a few ways to bridge the gap:

• *Find out why it's so hard to accept your children's choices when they're different from your own.* Use the hot buttons exploration described for teenagers (page 221), but ask yourself why you feel so strongly about this issue, why you need to be in control, and why you can't accept their right to make independent choices. This line of questioning may lead you back to the "Mirror, Mirror" exercise in chapter 8 (page 194).

• *Tap into the power of apology.* It's never too late to say "I'm sorry, I wish I could have been a better parent," "I wish I had done things differently," or "You deserved better than I gave." Heartfelt words of sadness and regret become particularly powerful in a letter—as long as the letter is given as a gift without expectations about what it will bring in return. It may bring nothing except the knowledge that you have done your best to right past wrongs, but you may also wish to ask if there is any way that you can make amends.

• *Explore what you expect from each other.* If your estranged child is willing, each of you should make a list of no more than seven items on the subject of what you want and need from each other and what you think the other wants and needs from you. Now compare lists and see how close each of you comes to meeting the other's needs.

If your child is unwilling or you're unwilling to ask, you can still do this exercise on your own. Fill out the list for yourself, then move to another chair or position and fill out a list as you think your adult child would. Now compare. Is what your adult child needs different from what you're offering? Have you failed to recognize how the child has changed?

When Roles Reverse: Using EQ During the Sandwich Years

Sometime in your life, possibly before your own children are fully independent, you may find your aging parents dependent on you as well. If you've let negative emotional memories fester, it might be hard to take care of Mom and Dad with loving generosity. Fortunately you have EQ to help you mend fences. Follow heartpath 8, admitting to error, and try the hot buttons technique. To give your parents what they need without giving up your life, follow heartpaths 9 and 10—discovering individual needs and generously expressing your love—as well as these suggestions:

• *Make sure the person in need feels needed, too.* Elderly individuals who suffer infirmities and are emotionally isolated commonly suffer depression. So do those who feel they're no longer contributing to the world. Can you convey to your parents that your family needs them as much as they need you? Can you find nontoken ways for your family to benefit from their unique abilities? If these efforts are inadequate, do you have the resources to encourage your parents to make a contribution outside the family? The need for volunteers to serve as literacy tutors, "foster" grandparents, civic leaders, and in a million other capacities never ends, but if doing that work requires help (like transportation), your parents may hesitate to ask for more from you. Try the "Personalizing the Meaning of Love and Support" exercise in chapter 7 (page 164) to see where your prospects for give and take lie. If your parents express boredom, why not share the exercises at the beginning of chapter 8 to help them explore what type of work would make them feel most fulfilled today?

• *Never give more than you can bear.* Unconsciously, if not consciously, we show those we love our true feelings, and when those feelings are mixed with anger and resentment, though it may be at the situation rather than the person, what gets communicated is anger and resentment. Remember heartpath 5 and take responsibility for all that you convey. Diligent active awareness will also keep you from tipping the scale toward martyrdom—you'll be able to stay on heartpath 4 by knowing exactly when you need to be on the receiving end instead of the giving end of the family continuum.

Empathy will tell you what your parents need, which may in fact be less than you think. If you rely on your mind rather than your body, don't be surprised if your parents never seem satisfied no matter how much you give. Could they be trying to tell you that you're not giving them what they really need?

You may want to begin with the direct approach and ask, "What makes you feel loved?" or "What can I do to make you feel good?" If your parents can't answer the question or they don't know, you can experiment. Try phoning regularly, faxing, writing, or sending funny cards and see what happens. Does a short visit once or twice a week mean the most? What about arranging for services like a massage? Do they like flowers? Do your parents appreciate a home-cooked meal, or would they rather be taken out to dinner? Or would they rather sit around with you and play a game of cards? Make it your business to find out, through creative experimentation, what really gives them pleasure. If they feel that what you are doing is for them, they'll feel loved. Again, the exercise in chapter 7 can help you determine what to give and take.

• *Be prepared to seek help.* If you're to avoid giving too much, practical reality may dictate that you find someone to fill in. Do you have siblings who can help? In many families one child ends up burdened by too great a share of the responsibility for aging parents. If you've stayed close with brothers and sisters, and all of you have a high EQ, you can always come up with solutions because everyone will be crystal clear on his or her heartfelt priorities. If you've drifted apart or suffered a rift for some other reason, the suggestions in the following section may help you get help from siblings. Otherwise, keep in mind that assistance is always out there somewhere:

• Hire someone to do some of the things that need to be done for your parents.

• Get help from one or more of the many service agencies that serve the elderly. You may need to use several to get the variety of help you need—transportation, food, legal and accounting, etc. Look up these resources in the Yellow Pages and remember that many local churches and synagogues have assistance programs and lists of individuals who are willing to help in various ways.

• Exchanges: Who do you know in your family or among your group of friends and acquaintances who might be willing to do you a favor for a favor in return? For example, your mother or father needs a ride to the doctor—can someone you know take your parent during the week if you baby-sit, cook, clean, type, do their books, etc., over the weekend? Or would a friend take care of your parents for a day if you took care of his or hers on another day?

Reclaiming Your Adult Siblings

In high-EQ families, brothers and sisters divide up responsibilities for aging parents and look forward to occasions to get all the generations together, because they all know their limits and their talents and how to convey them. Unfortunately this is not an accurate portrait of many adult sibling relationships because too often history intervenes. Maybe your parents didn't provide the type of love and support your brother needed as well as they did for you. Maybe childhood memories trigger too much resentment, jealousy, and rivalry. Maybe it just hurt too much when the sister who knew you so well didn't care enough to notice how you've changed over the years.

Whatever the problem, you can use any of the ideas in this chapter to renew your relationship. If you have the time, you can also try reconnecting by going away together where you will both be comfortable and undisturbed. Try an unstructured setting like a camping trip, a long hike, a trip to a spa, a fishing trip, etc., and use your time together to send a lot of "I feel" messages. Clarify that in expressing yourself you're not asking your sibling to change. When your sibling responds, make sure you listen with your body, not with retorts prepared in your head.

If your sibling is hard to reach, and an outing won't work, can you reconnect by soliciting help in a way that acknowledges his or her unique talents—on a volunteer project, for example?

This approach can also be helpful when you need an estranged sibling's help with your aging parents. How can you make the prodigal brother or sister feel uniquely needed? If your sibling is estranged because of a poor relationship with Mom and Dad, try wording your request as a request for help for you, not them. Avoid low-EQ directives like "You should . . ."

Weaving a Richer Tapestry: Your Extended Family

How are your relationships with your extended family—those you're related to by marriage or through looser blood ties? Strained because you're trying to form family bonds without the emotional history to make them stick? Or smooth because they don't come with the emotional baggage that your immediate family of origin drags around? Either is possible in any individual relationship. How difficult one of these relationships is may depend on how important it is to you and how long you've been at it. Getting along with a brand-new mother-in-law therefore might be trying, especially if your relationship with your own mother has left unpleasant emotional memories. On the other hand, it's probably a snap to be cordial to the cousin you see only at holiday gatherings.

How good and how deep your relationships are with extended family will depend largely on what you want them to be. We feel guilty if we resent our own parents, but there's nothing in the Bible that says we have to love our in-laws, so many people don't feel obligated to make a huge effort. I believe you are, however, obligated to extend the same empathy to your extended family as you would to anyone else you encounter, and that means accepting the broad range of differences that's bound to exist (heartpath 9) so you can find the common points of connection.

If you're also willing to listen with empathy no matter who is speaking (heartpath 2), admit error (heartpath 8), and watch the nonverbal cues you send (heartpath 5), you stand a pretty good chance of becoming everyone's favorite niece, cherished uncle, or model in-law. Assuming you haven't yet achieved that lofty state, here are a few tips to make extended-family relationships rewarding.

• *Remember that you don't have to like everyone equally.* Sometimes, even when you make your most open-hearted efforts, you end up disliking a relative or an in-law. Start by using the "Mirror, Mirror" exercise in chapter 8 to examine how much your own baggage keeps you from appreciating this person. Then accept your feelings and interact with the person only to the extent that you remain comfortable. You may find that removing the stress of seeing him or her under duress opens your heart a crack wider. Try the following research project.

WHERE DO THEY LIVE EMOTIONALLY?

Not everyone will be willing to disclose their deepest feelings to a relative stranger, but most people are thrilled to be asked about themselves, and this is often the only way to connect with someone you're having trouble getting close to. What you want to know is what feels loving to members of your extended family and what *they* perceive as their emotional wants and needs. To the degree that you're willing to pay attention and stay in your body, members of your extended family will disclose (verbally or nonverbally) what is important to them. Relaxed, unstructured settings invite questions like the following:

• What are your happiest childhood memories?
• What makes you feel special?
• What do you think makes people feel loved?

• *If you can only ask loaded questions, don't say anything at all.* Research has shown that the emotional message is 90 percent of what people get from any communication, and that's why it's important to be emotionally aware of what your motives are and to take responsibility for what you convey through gestures and expressions, as well as words (heartpath 5). Too often we don't say what we mean because we're afraid to take responsibility for the feelings that motivate us. So we manipulate people by making offers that beg to be refused or by saying we don't mind when we do and then resenting the perceived offender. If you can't be emotionally honest with your extended family, go somewhere else.

A Paradigm for Living Smart with Your Family

In their determination to give the best of themselves to their role as parents, Hank and Sally took parental leaves for several weeks after each of their children was born, then returned to work on flex schedules. Because they were in touch with what went on with their children during the day, they noticed that their middle child, Eric, didn't stick up for himself the way the other kids did. At first Sally tried to protect Eric by intervening in his behalf, but Hank questioned how he'd learn to stick up for himself that way, so the two brainstormed for a more constructive way to help Eric gain self-confidence. Because Eric was a small, physically awkward child, Sally and Hank decided to give him dancing lessons when he was three. He was the only boy in the dancing class, but he didn't notice—he just had fun. The movement strengthened him physically, and the music loosened him up, stimulating more outgoing behavior with the other children. By the time he was five, Eric could do simple gymnastics and handle himself well with other children. He began school with confidence and did well socially and scholastically.

Some of the best times Sally and Hank shared with their children were one-on-one events. Even on family vacations or outings, Sally and Hank made it a point to spend time alone with each child, talking, playing, or reading interactively. This practice paid dividends during the teenage years, when each child had very different individual needs. Their older son needed driving lessons that occasioned leisure time to talk man to man with his father. Eric had developed an interest in music, and Sally used the occasion of his evening music lessons to take him out to dinner and catch up on important events in his life. Sally and Hank's daughter, Marcia, a social butterfly, wasn't especially interested in either of them, but warmed to the attention of Sally's brother Steve.

Steve was nearly a dozen years younger than Sally. A favorite with all the family, he was especially adored by the kids, who saw him more as a peer than as an uncle. Steve was special in another way, too. He had contracted diabetes at an early age and gave himself two insulin shots every day of his life—a habit that occasioned family discussions on important subjects like health and death. When Steve married and left the city, the entire family suffered a real sense of loss.

As the years passed, Steve called and visited less and less frequently. He seemed unhappy in his marriage and resentful of Sally's success in life, and this hurt Sally. She too pulled back, and their contacts became perfunctory. Then came news that Steve's wife had walked out on him and he had lost his job. When Sally called to talk, he sounded so low that she got worried. "He seemed a little incoherent—a sign that he might not be managing his medication," she told Hank. Sally didn't know what to do. Her instinct was to drop everything, go to Steve, and ask him to come home with her, but she was afraid that his pride wouldn't permit him to come. Hank encouraged her to follow her heart and gut and suggested that she take Marcia. "You know how well the two of them got on—having Marcia there should ease things between the two of you."

On their way to Steve's, Sally told Marcia how deeply she regretted losing touch with her brother. Steve was such an important part of their family, she should have done more to preserve their relationship when he moved away. Now, when he was in trouble, she realized how much she loved him but wondered if she would be able to reach her brother. When Sally saw Steve, she knew that she had done the right thing in following her heart. Steve seemed to have lost his will to live. His color was bad, and he wasn't thinking clearly—a sign that his diabetes was dangerously out of control. She and Marcia took him to the emergency room of a local hospital, where he was immediately admitted. During the next few days, as Steve's condition stabilized, he and Sally talked about the hurts that had separated them and renewed their relationship. She persuaded him to relocate near her home and move in with her family until he got settled. Within a few months Steve found a job and an apartment.

The following year he remarried. "How can I ever repay you?" Steve asked Sally. "You saved my life." "You're my brother. There's nothing to repay," Sally replied.

Ten years later their mother, now a widow, was diagnosed with Alzheimer's disease. The signs had been evident for some time, but coming shortly after Sally's diagnosis of cancer the diagnosis was particularly devastating. Steve took the lead and told his sister, "I don't want you to worry; your job for the present is to focus exclusively on getting well. I'll take good care of Mother." And he did. With one child and a second on the way, the additional responsibility of figuring out what to do with his mother squeezed Steve's emotional resources, but he managed with help from local community service agencies. He investigated board and care facilities specializing in the care of people with dementia and chose one near his office. Before or after work almost every day he dropped in on his mom to say hello and make sure she was being treated well. The staff, noticing Steve's concern, was especially attentive to his mother. On weekends his family picked up Mom and took her to the movies or on a picnic, and the outings did her good.

Knowing that Steve was taking responsibility for their mother's care was an enormous source of support for Sally. "I'm so grateful," she told Steve. "I know just how you feel," he said. "You've done the same for me!"

Part 3

STAYING
SMART

10

❧

A 10-Step Curriculum for Emotional Wisdom

Here is a template you can superimpose on everyday life, throughout life. If your EQ is already high, you can use these ten steps as a reminder and a reference to keep you self-aware and self-fulfilled.

1. **Make care of your body a priority.**
   - ♥ Get enough rest—experts recommend seven and a half to eight hours a night. You can get along on less, but you won't function optimally.
   - ♥ Exercise, stretch, move, and tone. You don't have to become an exercise freak—20 or 30 minutes of exercise once or twice a day will bolster physical and emotional awareness.
   - ♥ What you eat affects how you feel emotionally and mentally as well as physically. Overeating and eating the wrong foods dull perceptions and emotional awareness.
2. **Search for feeling in your body, not your head.**
   - ♥ Emotion is a felt experience that occurs somewhere below the bridge of the nose.
   - ♥ Your emotions speak to you through the viscera and musculature of your body.

3. **Build emotional muscle every day by taking time to focus on emotional experience.**
   - ♥ Practice the Building Emotional Muscle process until it becomes second nature.
   - ♥ Live in the moment by sustaining emotional awareness in your everyday life.

4. **Be accepting of all that you feel.**
   - ♥ You can tolerate feelings you don't necessarily enjoy, provided you stay out of your head and in physical experience.
   - ♥ By accepting what you feel, you merge EQ with IQ.

5. **Open your heart to others.**
   - ♥ Take your capacity to feel into love, work, and family relationships.
   - ♥ Let your feeling resonate with the feeling of all others.

6. **Take action—do things that make you feel useful and relevant.**
   - ♥ Let feelings influence your choices.
   - ♥ Let feelings inspire your actions.

7. **Listen with your empathy.**
   - ♥ Listen to the feelings beneath the words.
   - ♥ Listen with your eyes, your heart, your stomach, and other body parts as well as your ears.

8. **Tell them how you feel.**
   - ♥ Deep feelings are a source of strength.
   - ♥ Messages sent from the heart penetrate intellectual barriers.

9. **Use change as an opportunity to grow.**
   - ♥ Passion gives you the energy to keep growing.
   - ♥ Passion gives you a means for enacting healing change.

10. **Take a dose of humor with you wherever you go.**
    - ♥ Laughter instantly balances head and heart.
    - ♥ Nothing gets you out of your head more quickly than a real belly laugh.

11

⁘

Graduation!

One of my greatest joys is witnessing how EQ broadens and deepens people's lives. I've looked on gratefully while friends and family have cemented relationships and found fulfillment. I've received letters and calls from people describing how emotional intelligence has transformed their lives and their outlook on life. I have personally experienced its power to overcome loss. And I'd love to know where you are now that you've reclaimed emotion from the archives of your personal resources.

One thing I'm sure of is that if you've put this book into practice your EQ is increasing every day. Lifetime growth is practically inevitable when you witness the benefits of EQ yourself, and it's not just emotional growth. What makes emotional intelligence so valuable as time goes by is that it makes our fragmented, compartmentalized selves whole again.

Whether we look to religion, philosophy, or some other external source, most of us instinctively seek a way to unify body, mind, and spirit. How ironic, then, that we should find the means to fulfillment, success in life, and health within ourselves! It makes perfect sense, of course. By stifling and numbing emotion we began to separate body from mind and both from spirit. By reawakening our feelings we naturally restore what was torn asunder. In the process we return to the fundamental truth that the whole self is made up of many equally important parts.

And it's taken us only about two thousand years to start living that truth again. Back around the first or second century B.C., Greek physician-priest Asclepiades understood that the human being was a multifaceted whole and that well-being depended on emotional, physical, and spiritual health. Before he would treat a patient, the ailing person had to go through introspective rituals to uncover personal imbalances and surmount irrational fears. But then we in the West lost our respect for the importance of harmonious inner balance. In turn we seemed to lose the intimate spiritual connection we were meant to have with the world around us.

It's gratifying to see that changing today. Holistic health practices, for example, are now held in increasingly high esteem by enlightened health care givers and consumers alike. And if you thought about it, I'm sure you'd be among them. After all, you should have been realizing the most immediate rewards of a higher EQ—greater energy, fewer illnesses, and increased vitality—for some time now. If you continue to use what you've learned in this book as a modern replacement for Asclepiades's rituals, you have even more to gain—physically, mentally, emotionally, and spiritually.

To begin with, your prospects for future physical health are enormous. Your physical awareness of changes taking place within you serves as an ever-vigilant early warning system, so you'll be able to head off many illnesses before you're overcome by them. A dancer I know was so sensitive to what was transpiring inside her that she was able to point doctors to the location of a tumor that was undiagnosable by ordinary medical means. I sincerely hope no serious health problems are in your future, but if they arise, your EQ will not only catch them early but also speed your recovery.

As a psychologist who has worked with physically ill people for over two decades in physicians' offices, clinics, hospices, private practice, training programs, and workshops, I've personally observed that people who feel strongly that they have something to live for have an advantage over those who concentrate only on overcoming illness. Research from the University of California supports my observations, and so does the leading-edge medical science psychoneuroimmunology, or PNI. Information that chemical messages operative in both the brain and the immune systems are most dense in neural areas regulating emotion supports what we've known for a long time—that emotional well-being determines whether someone who is seriously ill declines rapidly or thrives. There's so much data linking emotion with recovery from illness, in fact, that in his groundbreaking book *Emotional Intelligence,* Daniel Goleman advocates the integration of emotional intervention into standard medical care for all serious disease. I heartily concur and recommend the techniques in this book as a way to connect people to emotions that sustain hope, define meaning, and stimulate immune response.

These techniques not only help us battle illness but empower us to make health-preserving choices that add up to a lifetime of vitality. Do you need rest and nourishment right now, or can they wait while you pursue an exciting idea or activity? Have you substituted one draining job for another, one compulsive activity for something just as counterproductive? The ability to answer these questions accurately contributes hugely to a longer, more vital life.

Having come this far, you also know emotion's power to enhance your intellect. You've seen it in the mental clarity and concentration you have now that your emotions don't get in the way, and you've seen how feeling makes cognitive self-improvement techniques, such as those in chapters 7 to 9, not only more effective but enduring for the first time. With the brainpower they've gained I've seen people achieve everything from greater efficiency on the job to exciting new vocations and avocations.

Anything is possible when your EQ is high, not just because you're feeling good and thinking well but because emotion gives you boundless motivation to act. *Now you've found inside yourself the means to make your dreams come true.* It's the ultimate in power, expansive and incorruptible, because when you know how you feel you also know how others feel. Add empathy to passion, and you find yourself moved to act not only in your own behalf but in behalf of others, too. Using that power only adds to your knowledge of yourself and your fellow human beings and therefore to your constant emotional growth.

You've already been using EQ to resolve differences and conflicts of interest in intimate relationships, at work, and with your family. As you keep your EQ growing you'll find that the differences in feelings, desires, personalities, opinions, and values you encounter in other settings don't have to become divisive. EQ fosters respect, creativity, and camaraderie; it's the element that helps groups reach their constructive potential.

This fact struck me once when a selected group of caring, like-minded writers, psychologists, social scientists, and community leaders gathered to look for solutions to pressing social issues. Over the course of several days, whenever passions soared and tempers flared, the group facilitators abruptly intervened, ending the discussion. For example, when a nonwhite community leader politely asked why a speaker had referred to a group that was 80 percent white and mostly upper middle class as "diverse," one woman launched into a long monologue on forgiveness, which many felt was an avoidance of the very issues the group had convened to discuss. Before anyone could speak, however, the facilitators called an impromptu recess, and at the end of the break a completely new subject was introduced. So it went whenever a charged issue surfaced. Everyone became increasingly numb intellectually as well as emotionally. Not surprisingly, without passion to fuel it, creative problem solving was cut off before it ever began.

In contrast, when the subject of homelessness began to tear apart a prominent West Coast community, high EQ fostered a positive resolution. Divisions went deep and passions ran high as homeless advocates battled home and business owners for the rights of homeless people to panhandle on city streets and occupy city parks. To deal with the escalating conflict, the city created a task force that included all the representative elements in the community—business interests, home owners, social service providers, homeless advocates, and the homeless themselves. In this instance, however, the facilitators met first with each participant to identify the issues people on the task force felt passionate about. Participants were given guidelines encouraging them to broaden their understanding by listening and speaking from their emotions. A questionnaire was distributed that focused participants on their tone of voice, facial expressions, and other nonverbal cues. They were also asked to consider their style of communication in light of their culture: Were they apt to remain silent, speak aggressively, and so on?

Respect for feelings as well as ideas created a safe, relaxed context, and as empathy and understanding flourished, a common goal surfaced: to get as many people as possible permanently off the streets. By its conclusion, the task force had drafted a detailed plan that called for new housing supported jointly by the city and business interests, a shelter to be built with coordinated efforts by all social service providers, a nighttime park curfew, and new policies restricting panhandling. Within three years all of these objectives were met, and while some homeless people remained in the community, their numbers and associated problems dropped substantially.

The same principles of high EQ that help smaller groups resolve conflicts also apply to conflicts of interest involving more diverse groups. Facing people you fear from emotionally protective positions invites the escalation of fear and disunity. But listening and speaking with emotional awareness and empathy brings people together even when they seem worlds apart.

Feelings are great levelers among people. Most human beings approach the unfamiliar with fear and uncertainty, but when you can feel those fears in yourself *and* others, fear can't stand between you. Thus the gates are opened to compassion, and the more that you practice your emotional skills, the more sensitive you become to subtle feeling sensations that open spiritual dimensions in your life.

Active awareness and empathy strengthen your connections to people you don't know, to nature, and to the cosmos. Where once your life felt closed, exclusive, separate, and finite, with EQ you may feel open, inclusive, and infinite. Maybe you never enjoyed doing things for others. Now that your EQ has been raised, doing for others feels like accomplishing something for yourself. Strangers matter because your life is energized and sweetened by helping them feel better.

In fact, the scale of what you experience as family grows. Nature, animals, plants, flowers, birds—all become your relations. And just as spending intimate time with loved ones energizes and renews you, so do your experiences with this extended family.

The awareness that high EQ brings into your life may also include a closer relationship to the cosmos, God, or Goddess. Mysticism is universally experienced as an ecstatic feeling state that not only brings us closer to God but closer to ourselves and others. Saint Teresa of Avion, recognized as one of the greatest mystics of the Middle Ages, defined a genuine mystical experience as one that improves your relationship to yourself and others—the same way you use EQ to determine whether anything is genuinely good for you. Those who live passionately in relationship to themselves and others live close to God. In consequence they may also be less frightened by death. When you palpably feel like part of a greater whole, your self expands beyond the borders of your body and death seems less an ending than an adventure into another dimension.

I believe you gain a new dimension of experience when your EQ is high. Emotional intelligence acts as a kind of sixth sense with which you can link personal well-being to community, national, and global well-being. So if I've blurred the distinction between what you stand to gain emotionally from a lifetime of EQ and what you stand to gain spiritually, perhaps that's because I honestly don't know where one ends and the other begins. What matters, in any case, is that the infinite capacity to love and be loved, to give and to receive, can change anyone's life without changing external events and influences one whit.

Celia: A Lesson for Us All

Celia taught me that lesson nearly twenty-five years ago. Newly graduated, I had begun working for a large agency that provided social services for families. Here I first encountered people like Celia who moved through life "in limbo," attempting to accept their misery. Professionals at the agency dealt with their frustration with these sad people by labeling them as having psychological disorders that prevented them from healing. It seemed to me that most of their problems were situational rather than medical or psychological. I reasoned that if somehow I could help them build a stronger sense of self-worth, perhaps their lives could be improved.

Before I met Celia, I was given a bulging file that told a story of lifelong neglect. At our first meeting, Celia's appearance confirmed the description of parental abandonment, isolation, hopelessness, and despair that filled the pages of her file. Celia's sagging frame, her blotchy, loose skin, and her frightened, darkly circled eyes made her seem older than her fifty-three years.

Celia was a "regular" at the agency. For nearly a decade, she had been seeing a counselor, but little had changed in her life. As the newest person on staff, it was my responsibility to take over old, "slow-moving" cases. Once again, Celia detailed the story that she had already shared with four other therapists, a story of poverty and neglect.

Celia's early life was spent in the deep South with a succession of foster parents. Her most treasured early memory was of being given a cup of tea and a few kind words when she was ill. Apparently this was the only tenderness and recognition she had received as a child. Celia married a man who also showed very little interest in her. The marriage produced no children. For thirty-five years, she had functioned more like a full-time, live-in housekeeper than like a wife.

Through all she experienced, Celia remained emotionally aware. She neither silenced, intellectualized, nor ignored her emotions. Sadness, loneliness, and fear were active parts of her life. Much about the world terrified and overwhelmed Celia. She didn't drive and had no intention of learning. Traffic, busy shopping centers, high altitudes, and unfamiliar situations made her anxious. Because experiences were often accompanied by panic attacks, Celia stayed close to home.

After years of therapy, Celia was well aware of the emptiness in her marriage. However, she was unwilling to abandon the security of having food on the table and a roof over her head. Independence offered no more than what she had experienced as a child and perhaps even greater hardship. Poorly educated, phobic, and physically and emotionally unhealthy after a lifetime of neglect, Celia saw little chance of turning her life around.

My meetings with Celia produced no new revelations. In soft tones, she conveyed the monotony of uneventful days spent cleaning, cooking, and watching TV. I attempted to listen with fresh interest each week, but I found myself growing drowsy as I heard the repeated negativity and predictability of her story.

I turned to my supervisor for help. He assured me that I was doing all that could be done by listening to her, but I didn't feel reassured. Celia was 53, not 93. Her teeth were bad, and she had more than her share of aches and pains, but if she wanted, she could live for another twenty-five years. How was Celia going to use that time? Was her weekly therapy session going to be the highlight of her week for the next twenty-five years? What kind of life was that?

In desperation, I looked around for something—anything— that might give Celia a glimmer of excitement and hope. On the way to my office one morning, I noted a sign on the door of another service provider in the same building. "The Volunteer Bureau," it said. I was intrigued and went inside. There I was told that over 10,000 requests for volunteer service were on file. All people had to do was to state their interests and availability, then they would receive the names of several organizations needing volunteer help. When I first broached the subject of becoming a volunteer, Celia was wary. "I'm afraid I won't be good and

I don't have anything to offer," she said. "Besides, I don't like to travel too far from home."

"If you don't enjoy the work, don't do it," I told her, "but there are people whose lives you can help. Are you willing to explore the possibility that you have something to offer that could make a difference to others as well as make your life better?"

Celia thought about the suggestion for several weeks before going downstairs to investigate the Volunteer Bureau. Her feelings were a mixture of fear and curiosity. The bureau director asked Celia where her interests lay, and she told him, "Children, all ages." There were requests for help from an orphanage and from several day-care programs, but these didn't involve working directly with children.

"Do you have any skills?" the director asked. "For example, do you perhaps sew?"

To my complete surprise Celia answered, "Yes, I like to sew." In all the material recorded about Celia's life there wasn't a single reference to her interest in sewing.

The bureau director told us that there was an urgent request from a home for unwed mothers for someone to teach sewing to their pregnant teenagers. Apparently only a few secondhand sewing machines were available to the institution's clients, but there was great interest in and a need for making maternity and infant clothing.

"Make do" and "hand-me-down" were ways of life that Celia knew well, having lived with those conditions as she grew up. "I'll try it," Celia said, agreeing to take a bus trip across town for the first time in years. Buoyed by a desire to help, and aware that she could get off the bus and return home at any time, Celia screwed up her courage and ventured into crosstown traffic. She had to relax her hold on certainty and take a step into the unknown, but her longing to do something that she cared about propelled her forward.

Fortunately, she was immediately put to work in a way that fulfilled her expectations. The pregnant teenagers Celia met that first day were scarcely more than children themselves. Some were as young as 13 or 14, and many had pasts like her own. The young women she met were poor and desperately needed clothing.

My hope for Celia turned into excitement as I saw her become increasingly absorbed in her activities for "the home." Because there were only a few rickety sewing machines and the class was large, Celia was drawn into conversation while the girls waited their turn to use the machines. Celia developed friendships and began spending two days each week as a volunteer.

Her days away from the home were spent investigating fabric sales or finding patterns that could be used in the class. The more skilled and confident her students became, the more useful and important Celia felt. Our conversations reflected this growing confidence. Celia no longer talked obsessively about the emptiness in her own life. Instead, she spoke of the girls with whom she worked each week. The passing parade of mothers-to-be became Celia's first real family. The young women, too, grew fond of Celia, and several asked her to be present during the birth of their babies. Celia stayed in touch with many of the girls, sometimes baby-sitting for those who chose to keep their babies. One young woman even named her daughter Celia, after the teacher and friend she admired.

Although no major changes occurred in her external environment, Celia now experienced her life in a totally different way. She did things that mattered to others and in so doing created a meaningful life for herself. Each morning she awakened with an anticipation of important work to be done. People were counting on her to solve problems that required ingenuity. Perhaps for a few dollars she could purchase an old sewing machine in good repair or find good buttons on old clothing at a garage sale. These challenges and opportunities brought Celia new hope and excitement.

I now enjoyed talking to Celia and being with her. Ironically, as I found our meetings increasingly interesting, Celia began losing interest in therapy. *Living* life had become more interesting than *talking* about it.

I hope that will be true for you.